In Search of Cricket

IN SEARCH OF CRICKET

J. M. KILBURN

Introduction by Matthew Engel

THE PAVILION LIBRARY

First published in Great Britain in 1937

Copyright © J. M. Kilburn 1937
Introduction copyright © Matthew Engel 1990

First published in the Pavilion Library in 1990 by
PAVILION BOOKS LIMITED
196 Shaftesbury Avenue
London WC2H 8JL

Series Editor: Steve Dobell

A CIP catalogue record for this book
is available from the British Library

ISBN 1 85145 486 1 Hbk
ISBN 1 85145 491 8 Pbk

Printed and bound in Great Britain by
Biddles Limited, Guildford

INTRODUCTION

I started reading *In Search of Cricket* after a British Rail breakfast on a train between King's Cross and Leeds, which was the perfect setting. It is a book written by a Yorkshire cricket-writer, largely but not entirely about Yorkshire cricket, and first published in 1937. It is very much a book of its time and place – perhaps THE book.

It has become rather fashionable to read cricket reports and essays of the 1930s, or at least to read the reports of one man: Sir Neville Cardus. The Cardus nostalgia industry, which has just stopped short of selling souvenir knick-knacks and T-shirts, has reached almost alarming proportions; for modern readers his brilliant but idiosyncratic view of the '30s has become received wisdom.

J. M. – Jim – Kilburn represents an equal but opposite tradition. In 1934, when Cardus was well entrenched at the *Manchester Guardian*, Kilburn took over as cricket correspondent of the *Yorkshire Post*. He remained in the job until 1976. That is astonishing service; John Woodcock did over 30 years as correspondent of *The Times* and E. W. Swanton did 29 on the *Telegraph*. Modern cricket correspondents, worn out by travel, are lucky to last five. Even allowing for the hiatus of the war, and the fact that he was not on the county circuit much towards the end, Kilburn's record of durability must be hard to beat. In his later years, he became a sort of embodiment of the Yorkshire tradition, at a time when it was faltering.

Kilburn was 25 when he was appointed. He had been to Sheffield University, done a little schoolmastering and then, through friends, spent a winter in Finland whence he sent the *Post* a few travel articles. He came back and asked for a job. The editor, Arthur Mann, was a keen cricketer; Kilburn was well-known in the office because they often printed his name in the Bradford League reports as a useful bowler of medium-paced off-breaks who batted a bit. The cricket job had not been properly filled since the retirement of A. W. Pullin – a writer of the florid Edwardian school who used the pseudonym 'Old Ebor' – three years before. And so it happened: six months' probation at £3 a week. Kilburn knew nothing of the details of daily journalism. That was no handicap.

Across the Pennines there was Cardus, a cricket-writer full of glorious improvised strokes but sometimes a little suspect in defence. Now Yorkshire had Kilburn, much more of a grafter. He was not without deft touches of his own, as *In Search of Cricket* shows. But he represented – and became the epitome of – a different, harder school of cricket-writing. Cardus later skittered round various papers before finishing back on the *Guardian*, then removed to London. Kilburn never left the *Post* and the *Post* never left Yorkshire; both ideas were unthinkable.

Kilburn's father was a bank manager and it had always been a *Times* rather than a *Guardian* family. He had grown up on Bernard Darwin's sports-writing, but never aped anyone. That was appropriate for a man in his position. The provincial morning newspaper in the '30s had a special status in the community (the chief reporter of the *Yorkshire Post* wore a bowler hat and spats). Since then, most have either closed or declined. In Yorkshire cricket, though, the *Post's* pre-eminence has remained unchallenged, and that may well be Kilburn's major achievement.

He developed a punctilious method of writing, which he stuck to with exceptional determination. He wrote with a fountain pen very neatly on Press Telegram forms – 60 words a shilling or 80 words a shilling, cheap rate after six o'clock. After the war, the telephone came in, but that was not for Kilburn. He asked for – and carried enough clout to be given – a telephonist on each ground to dictate his words for him. The modern method by which journalists have to use their own portable computers would be incomprehensible to him.

Towards the end of his career, the quality of the *Yorkshire*

Post-issue copy paper deteriorated and he gave up the fountain pen in favour of a ball-point. That was just about his only concession. He still wrote everything out in longhand as the day went on, hardly ever crossed anything out and hardly joined in the traditional press-box discussion about what had happened on the field even after his traditional post-lunch nap. He knew his own mind.

That certainty extended to his journalistic method. He was never much interested in newspapers as such. As far as Kilburn was concerned, the cricket correspondent's job was to report what happened on the field. The idea of what he calls 'keyhole journalism' horrified him. A modern cricket-writer on a respectable paper feels the same, but long ago accepted that part of the job was to report something of the game's politics. Kilburn would have none of that; at 6.30 he concluded his essay, put his pen down and called for the telephonist. He lasted long enough for his ideas to seem quaint to both his colleagues and his editors, who started sending him plaintive missives about the need to compete with the *Daily Mail*; it is a tribute to his standing that he did not have to compromise.

The job began to lose some of its appeal, however, partly because of this kind of pressure and partly because the game itself was changing: no one can write an essay on a Sunday League match – well, one essay maybe, but hardly two and certainly not 16 a summer. Yorkshire's decline, after their last Championship, worried him less. With his historical perspective, he was especially well-equipped to analyse what was going wrong.

He was 80 in 1989, still lucid and exact. My picture of him is that of an upright, very dignified old man. After his retirement, failing eyesight turned to blindness and his contact with cricket now is at one remove. He prefers to hear his Test matches on the TV rather than the radio because he finds all the jocularity irritating. This did not entirely surprise me. He cut a famously aloof figure amidst the banter of the press-box.

Yet he is not a humourless man and *In Search of Cricket* is not a humourless book. Kilburn himself thinks he wrote much better later on. But there is a freshness about it that could only come from a young writer. It is a collection that mixes cricket reports with descriptive essays and tales of his travels with 'Michael' – in reality his colleague John Bapty of the *Evening Post*. The style of these has not always weathered well, and at times veers a little to the manner of the gushing guidebooks of Arthur Mee. But it is, as I say, of its time and, as such, unfailingly evocative.

His cricket-writing remains excellent. It is like a very Yorkshire innings, full of textbook defensive shots leavened with the occasional perfectly-executed cover-drive. Thus, of the short boundaries at Tonbridge: 'a well-hit six can drop with a thrilling crash upon hard slates'; and 'Grimmett, of course, had to come back to look into this situation but Ames played the ball and not the bowler's name'; and 'Leyland's bowling is mostly a joke, but it is an extremely practical joke'. This represents masterful control of the language.

There is very warm writing about the Yorkshire players of that era – note especially the description of Herbert Sutcliffe batting in a trilby. And towards the end, there is a particularly fine account of Yorkshire being bowled out for 31 at Huddersfield. It is almost three pages into the piece before the name of the triumphant opposition is actually mentioned. Only an old-time Yorkshire cricket-writer would attempt this. Only Kilburn could have done it and still made the piece readable, authoritative and definitive.

The cricket world has moved on and so have newspapers. It is hard to imagine Jim Kilburn, who for years resisted the innovation of a television in the press-box, doing the job now, though for years it was impossible to imagine Yorkshire without him. I asked him if he would do it all again today. He thought not, but added: 'While I have had the best of cricket in my lifetime, there will be lifetimes to come when it will be good enough.'

London, 1990   Matthew Engel

IN SEARCH OF CRICKET

By

J. M. KILBURN

To E. J. K. —
A Cricketer

CONTENTS

I am indebted to the Editor of *The Yorkshire Post* for permission to republish many of the following sketches, which had their first innings upon the very helpful wicket of that great newspaper.

J. M. K.

A PILGRIMAGE FOR THE FAITHFUL

IT is a pleasant fancy, though one I hold and am prepared to defend without claiming any originality for it, that cricketers are products of their environment and grow as they do grow because of the impulse in their setting. Illustrations beyond counting come flocking to the mind and I should but seek to 'gild refined gold' were I to stress the point with laboured argument.

To know Woolley at the crease is to know the calm maturity of sunlit Kentish meadows, to watch Tate shambling to the wicket is to meet the sunburned countryman plodding a brave way across the Sussex Downs, to contemplate Arthur Mitchell in the acquisition of an unsmiling, purposeful century is to appreciate the hard, unyielding Yorkshire hills which stand so sure of themselves and of their strength.

You do not make a cricketer only with bat and ball; a machine can be induced to deliver a ball, another to strike it, but that is not cricket or the essence of a cricketer. The cricketer is made from within, and his spiritual power is no conglomeration of surrounding atmosphere. To know cricket, therefore, is to know something of the world in which cricket is played, and many less worthy pilgrimages

have been made than that which leads through the
cricketer's England.

On such a journey the traveller might pass from
the cool sanctuaries of Canterbury across the

"Blunt, bow-headed, whale-backed Downs".

where shadows of fleeting clouds chase each other
throughout long summer days, to the sleepy, quiet-
breathing fields of Somerset; from Gloucester's vil-
lages across the Cotswold Hills to England's heart,
where Warwick's castles hold an ancient sway, to the
pleasant dales and much less pleasant towns of York
and Derbyshire; across the lawns of Aigburth even
to the rain and murk of Manchester.

This is no course for hurry; the pilgrimage must
take its time, and the traveller be content to spend
his day here, his week-end there, breathing deeply
everywhere and thinking himself blessed always.
Cricket is not altogether an easy taskmaster to the
traveller; wickets are pitched at the appointed hour
whether journeys be short or long, close of play is
unheeding of the call of the wind on the heath. Yet
cricket itself is not without memorable settings, and
from a seat on the boundary edge a surprising amount
of England's story can be read. You may watch bat
and ball at Worcester against a background filled
by one of our noblest cathedrals; almost you can see
the ruins of a Norman keep from the pavilion
balcony at Scarborough; with a little imagination
the tramp of the Second Legion of the Roman

Expeditionary Force comes to your ears during the intervals at Gloucester, and at Oxford or Cambridge you can scarcely avoid contact with the hours of yesterday.

Not all of England's story is written in bricks and mortar or in memories; the dignified neighbour who borrows your scorecard at Bath is a living tradition from another, less hurried, century; the accent of the local from whom you inquire the way is illustration for the book whose beginning is forgotten and whose ending is outside conjecture. No less important than the traveller's sight is his hearing and his speech.

In the matter of asking the way I have always considered myself particularly unfortunate; rarely do I stop to make inquiries without hitting upon the one deaf stroller in the roadway, or hearing a muttered, 'Sorry, I'm a stranger here myself.' Even a policeman failed me once. That was when Michael and I were forced into a hurried journey from Yorkshire into Worcestershire along unknown ways. Michael has been the companion of so many of my most pleasant trips; as driver or passenger he is without peer, but he has, or rather he had, an all-too-simple faith in the goodness of heart of those whose delight it is to plan out routes for other people to pursue. This time he held detailed information, that was, no doubt, thoroughly well meant, and would, no doubt, have been thoroughly adequate for a daylight journey of leisure, but as darkness fell upon us in the

Midlands, one road became indistinguishable from another and signposts grew fewer and fewer. Boredom and irritation settled upon driver and passenger alike until finally complete confusion was admitted.

Somewhere in the Black Country (and how black it is after modern curfew, which is the end of the cinema performances !), we found a policeman pacing in solitary state upon a gloomy pavement.

We drew up for inquiry.

Kidderminster, I believe, was our immediate objective, and with that politeness which the law commands in motorists we said so. The policeman, nodding gravely, admitted cognizance of Kidderminster; it was, apparently, off his beat, but he assured us that if we proceeded to the top of an invisible hill there were then several routes we might follow.

No, he could not exactly recommend any of them, though he knew that none was well spoken of. Bravely we asked for some estimate of distance.

'Well,' said the policeman, 'I wouldn't like to commit myself.'

Not all our assurances upon the preservation of confidences and the lack of necessity for swearing oaths upon the subject could induce that policeman to hazard an opinion. The caution of the witness-box remained triumphant, and we drove on unsatisfied in search of journey's end and eventual beer and sandwiches in Worcester.

MAY DAYS

THE opening of each cricket season is a voyage of most joyous adventure, for it brings promise of the thrilling unknown, together with the prospect of sailing again certain charted and well-loved seas. We go again where we have so often been before to find new paint upon the same pavilion railings, to see new figures tread the old steps well-worn by the feet of the mighty ones of yesterday. We go to see new faces, hear new names, yet still the game remains the same, the fresh and the mellow mingling and sweet.

The early days are always exciting, for form is uncertain and wickets a maze of bewildering contradiction; though May days of adventure are, paradoxically, not for youth but for sober experience. Every year the same story is told; the young cricketer comes eagerly forth, bat in hand, pads and boots gleaming white, and passes, a moment later, on his chastened way back to the pavilion, victim of mistiming or prey to cunning spin.

His elder colleague comes more quietly to the field. There is less downright challenge in his step and lovingly he feels the soft turf once more beneath his feet, drinks in the pale sunshine and breathes the spring air in quiet appreciation. This man knows that his innings are now numbered, feels that his remaining seasons are precious, and calls upon the impetuous failures of yesterday to help him along his present way. The old ones, the wise ones, make runs in May days, for they have known other Mays and feel within themselves that they cannot, as cricketers, know many more.

As May turns into June and the hard wickets of July and August follow, all batsmen worthy the name will make runs, for high summer is the batsmen's delight and all Nature gives him assistance. That is why youth perseveres; that is why to-day's failures are borne as patiently as may be—'I did not score to-day, but later in the season there will come a time . . .'

Not infrequently we have to suffer for our early cricket enthusiasm; spring days are not always fair and spring airs not always balmy as the poets would have us believe. 'Rain stopped Play' is a common cry when the English season begins. Sometimes mackin-toshes alone are not enough to keep warmth and comfort in spectators; great-coats and scarves, remin-iscent of football days, can often be seen mingling with white flannels and even the greatest enthusiasts have been known to watch the play from within the sphere of influence of the Long Room fire.

Perhaps the season of 1935 must be awarded the highest honour or infamy as the bringer of the coldest May that ever froze a suffering fieldsman.

Then not a single Oldest Member, wrapped in his overcoat and fixed immovably in the warmest corner, was heard to grumble in scorn, 'Cold, sir? Pah! Why, in 1868 when we played the Bohemians there was seven inches of snow in the outfield, and when I clean bowled F. W. V. Coates-Bedlington with the loveliest off-break you every saw, sir, I was robbed—robbed, I say, sir—of my just reward, because the bails were frozen to the stumps and refused to drop. That *was* cold, sir. You moderns are soft and pampered.'

The cricketers of 1935 will have a tale of hardihood to tell to their grandchildren, and the tale, no doubt, will lose nothing in the telling.

Through all those bitter winds with snowflakes scurrying from leaden skies cricket seemed unreal, an unkindly mockery of a kindly game. Batsmen came to the wicket muffled in scarves and hampered by as many sweaters as friends and fortune could bestow.

Bowlers started their work by peeling off two outer layers and then proceeded to the job still be-sweatered. No man could say a word against them: in the ordinary way to bowl in a sweater looks as wrong as to play in brown boots, but this was out of the ordinary way in cricket, and players were justified in going to any lengths to preserve some semblance of comfort and some possibility of blood circulation.

But for most bad springs there is a good one in store, and poor cricketing days will find somewhere a

compensating balance.   Good or bad, spring days
bring light hearts, for with cricket of any sort before
us again, life begins anew, dark winter fades to dark
oblivion, and the merest speck of blue in the sky is
enough to send us eagerly down the road on our way
to the ground.

KENTISH MEN

FOR centuries Tonbridge has lain quietly dreaming in the enchanted garden of Kent. Even now in this bustling twentieth century it is only in the main street, where the through traffic comes hurrying through, that movement is other than leisurely and contemplative. Summer days are sweet and shining with peace in Tonbridge, and cricket week is the crown of the year.

There are prettier cricket grounds than that at Tonbridge, for although there are trees and cool tents and fluttering flags, dull cottage roofs can be seen on two sides and the pavilion's sole beauty lies in its utility. Yet Tonbridge sees and is essentially part of true Kentish cricket. There the boundaries are not so far distant as to suggest their attainment being beyond mortal consideration, and a well-hit six can drop with a thrilling crash upon hard slates. Forbidding railings do not separate all the spectators from the players, and it is possible to watch cricket in that most delectable of ways, seated on the grass and willing and anxious to save perspiring and beaten fieldsmen a certain amount of toil.

Years ago there must have been a time when there was no cricket in Tonbridge; then, perhaps, there would be dancing and merrymaking and the pleasant jostling of crowds upon the castle green, over which you can still walk in the cool of the evening and dream and dream of men and maidens who strolled there long ago.

When cricket was in its swaddling clothes, Tonbridge came to know the game, and to-day it is a nursery for Kentish cricketers of promise and ambition. To learn cricket at Tonbridge is to come very near to earthly paradise, for every breeze that blows and every sun that glows brings the spirit and tradition of the game. The science of cricket has perhaps to be taught even in Tonbridge, but the life of the game needs no telling; it is part of the air of the place, and to be born in Tonbridge is to be already half a cricketer.

Woolley was born at Tonbridge and born in the month of May; how much of his genius, how much of the magic that is within him, and which he has called forth for our delectation these thirty years is dependent upon those two simple facts? Would Woolley, a Lancastrian, and seeing the first light in a drear December have been the Woolley we treasure so dearly?

It is impossible to separate the place and the men. There can be no grimness, no dour fighting when the environment is all mixed green, and blue and gold. Other counties, stern and points-wary at home, become transformed in Kent, and even Yorkshire scored more than 160 runs before luncheon on the first day when once they came beneath the spell.

Kent cricket is invariably an adventure; think of the Kentish men of cricket immortality, and at once you picture them in their own setting, batting with a smile upon sunburnt faces or bowling with smooth rhythm and gentle courtesy. Dillon, Day, Woolley, Hutchings, Seymour—the very names are poetry in themselves, and as for their achievements, was ever more perfect a living poem than dark-haired Kenneth Hutchings at the wicket or in the field?

One name, perhaps above all, means Kent and means Tonbridge. If, at the close of the day's play, you leave the ground and walk along the main street, crossing the almost motionless stream of the Medway, you will come to an alley way leading to the door of the Parish Church.

Here you must enter and go down the south aisle to the corner set apart for the children, and there on the wall read these words, graven on a tablet of stone :—

IN MEMORY OF COLIN BLYTHE, THE CELEBRATED KENTISH CRICKETER, THIS TABLET IS PLACED BY HIS SORROWING WIDOW AND HIS MANY FRIENDS IN KENT. HE PLAYED FOR ENGLAND AT HOME AND IN AUSTRALIA AND IN SOUTH AFRICA. HE WAS THE MAINSTAY OF THE KENT XI, FROM 1899 TO 1914.

IN SEPTEMBER, 1914, HE VOLUNTEERED AND WAS
ENROLLED IN THE KENT FORTRESS ENGINEERS, AND IN A
SHORT TIME PROMOTED TO BE SERGEANT.
IN 1917 HE WAS TRANSFERRED TO THE KING'S OWN
YORKSHIRE LIGHT INFANTRY, AND FELL IN ACTION AT
YPRES 8 NOVEMBER, 1917. ÆT 38.
AS CRICKETER, SOLDIER, AND PATRIOT HE PLAYED
THE GAME.
"GLORIFY GOD IN YOUR BODY."

And beneath these words is the banner of Kent with
'Invicta' standing clear.

Just as tears come to Australians' eyes when
Victor Trumper is mentioned, so is the name of
Colin Blythe revered through all Kent. He was the
darling of his day, supreme master of his art, and,
bowling, a sight as beautiful as any ever cricket has
known. He will never be matched, and as the years
drift by his memory will become more gloriously
enshrined in those who knew him by sight and by
story. This will be his memorial, deeper and wider
and more lasting than a cross in Flanders or a tablet
in a Tonbridge church.

As the epitome of Kent cricket, Colin Blythe will
never die.

THE BEST OF THE SEASON

BRADFORD, *1st June,* 1935.

THERE was an astonishing day's cricket here to-day; both sides completing an innings and Yorkshire finding themselves 51 runs behind. Yorkshire must have been reasonably satisfied when Kent were out for 182, but as Verity and Macaulay had shared six of the wickets, there was always the possibility that Freeman and Lewis would be equally awkward.

They proved even more deadly, for apart from Sutcliffe and Hutton no batsman could so much as attempt to deal with them, and the Yorkshire innings after tea was such a procession as to make all the more remarkable the forties of the opening pair. If all this happens on the first day, what has Monday in store?

Kent are a team of chivalrous batsmen. They were bowled out by Yorkshire for 182 runs to-day, and there was at one time every probability that they would be bowled out for considerably less, but that did not prevent them making good, strong shots and dying, when die they must, with a smile and a joke.

Smailes began their troubles within ten minutes of the start of play when Fagg, playing back without ever being very near the line of flight of the ball, was bowled, and there were but 23 runs on the board when Bowes turned one back to beat Ashdown's uncertain bat, and the middle stump became limp and drooping.

In the meantime beauty had come to the wicket, for Woolley, with a gleaming white bat, had hit Smailes straight and to leg for boundaries gathered with that negligent ease possessed only by Woolley in present-day cricket. Quietly and calmly this genius of Kent collected 33 runs, swinging Smailes beyond the leg boundary and forcing the ball off his pads in such comfort, that there was surprise and genuine disappointment (even amongst staunch Yorkshiremen) when at 48 he was lbw to Macaulay.

Woolley walked back to the pavilion in silent contemplation and with solemn steps and slow; equally slowly came Todd to the wicket, but whereas Woolley was probably wondering how he came to miss the fatal ball, Todd was gathering his mental resources for a fighting effort as cool and calculating as any ever played by Yorkist or Lancastrian.

Ames had little to say to the bowling (whatever may have been his private opinion concerning its unkindly accuracy), and at twenty-five minutes to one Bowes made one jump and Ames turned hurriedly away. The next ball was well up, but Ames chose to play back and was deservedly bowled, Kent's score thereupon reading 56 for four wickets.

To join Todd and blend stolidity with thrust

came Valentine; no idle, stay-and-wait-for-things-to-happen man was this, and by one o'clock 100 runs were made, Valentine having hit Macaulay amongst the pavilion spectators for 6. Nor was this his best shot, for once or twice he forced the ball superbly from his legs, and then he picked upon a slow long-hop from Verity and hooked it far away to crash against the wall.

But Valentine drank to intoxication this wine of his own making, and at quarter-past one Verity had him neatly and quickly stumped.

Chapman, veritable cavalier of cricketers, had neither caution nor fortune, and hit Bowes, at deep mid-off, a simple catch with the total 120.

At 123 it was lunch-time, and if Kent were satisfied I have no doubt that Yorkshire were equally so.

Levett had neither scored nor attempted to score at the interval, and he was still wanting a run when he pushed a ball straight to Sellers at silly mid-off and went his way. Verity was always Wright's master, and at 140 had him stumped, and 10 runs later Freeman hit across and skied a catch back to the bowler.

Now Kent, we said, are chivalrous cricketers, and when Lewis came in as last man, Todd was still in need of a run or two for his 50. No more was needed; Lewis stayed and stayed in comparative comfort, until at three o'clock, Todd made that 50.

By this time Lewis found that he rather liked staying, and not even the introduction of Bowes into the attack altered his opinion, so that 32 runs were added, and it was twenty-five minutes past three before Sutcliffe held a slip catch to finish off the innings.

Now a total of 182 was not to be despised, for there had been signs that the wicket looked better than it played, and there were those who foresaw a thorn or two in Yorkshire's path. Whether Sutcliffe and Hutton believed this and were playing to a pre-conceived plan or whether they merely took what they could in the ordinary way we do not know, but we were treated to the start of an innings such as we have not known before this season.

Hutton was delightful, and surely delighted. To begin with he had a boundary with a perfectly timed hook, and then in quick succession, came three 4's by way of glorious off-drives. No man could have improved upon these shots, and the whole of the Kent bowling resources had been called upon to no avail, when Hutton, playing a forcing back-shot, hit his wicket. This was cruel luck, for if ever a batsman deserved numerical reward for innings it was this one on this occasion. Forty-two may not seem a great score in next year's Wisden, but we who watched will not forget.

Yorkshire had a bad period after tea, for within half an hour Mitchell, Barber, and Leyland were all out, and Yorkshire not yet 100. Mitchell was stumped by yards, Leyland bowled off his pads, and Barber leg-before, all for 16 runs between them, and of these 15 belonged to Leyland for two or three hard drives.

Freeman and Lewis were now turning the ball appreciably, and batting was a matter of supreme good luck or supreme skill. Sellers stayed to see the 100 up and might have stayed a good deal longer than he did had he not been so delighted at pulling Freeman to the leg-boundary that he must needs essay a repetition and drop the ball into the hands of the waiting Valentine.

Through all these troublous times, Sutcliffe sat tight, answering his ill-advised critics by offering his bat. There were no acceptors, and Sutcliffe was left to hold up one end until Freeman turned one incredibly, the ball spun off the edge, and Woolley held a quick left-handed catch.

How great was the work of Sutcliffe and Hutton can be adequately gauged from the performances of the others; Verity, Smailes and Macaulay had but one shot between them—that a straight drive by Smailes—and the whole innings was over at 6.20.

KENT
First Innings

Ashdown, b Bowes	. . . . .	8
Fagg, b Smailes	. . . . .	0
Woolley, lbw, b Macaulay	. . . .	33
Ames, b Bowes	. . . . .	11
Todd, not out	. . . . .	63
B. H. Valentine, st Wood, b Verity	. .	35
A. P. F. Chapman, c Bowes, b Macaulay	. .	1
W. H. V. Levett, c Sellers, b Verity	. .	0
Wright, st Wood, b Verity	. . . .	6
Freeman, c and b Verity	. . . .	6
Lewis, c Sutcliffe, b Leyland	. . .	3
B. 4, l.b. 10, n.b. 2	. . .	16
Total	. . . . .	182

YORKSHIRE
First Innings

Sutcliffe, c Woolley, b Freeman	. . .	44
Hutton, hit wkt, b Freeman	. . .	42
Mitchell, st Ames, b Lewis	. . .	1
Leyland, b Lewis	. . . . .	15
Barber, lbw, b Freeman	. . . .	0
A. B. Sellers, c Valentine, b Freeman	. .	16
Wood, not out	. . . .	5
Verity, lbw, b Freeman	. . . .	0
Smailes, lbw, b Lewis	. . . .	5
Macaulay, st Ames, b Lewis	. . .	0
Bowes, st Ames, b Freeman	. . .	3
Total	. . . .	131

BOWLING ANALYSIS
KENT
First Innings

	o.	m.	r.	w.		o.	m.	r.	w.
Bowes	15	2	38	2	Verity	18	4	47	4
Smailes	9	0	36	1	Leyland	1	0	1	1
Macaulay	19	6	44	2					

Bowes and Macaulay each bowled a no-ball.

YORKSHIRE
First Innings

	o.	m.	r.	w.		o.	m.	r.	w.
Ashdown	5	4	8	0	Freeman	23·2	8	47	6
Todd	3	0	13	0	Lewis	20	6	45	4
Wright	4	0	18	0					

Umpires : Baldwin and Braund.

SECOND DAY

Yorkshire won a memorable match at 5.35 to-day, when they beat Kent by two wickets. Thrilling as were the varying fortunes of the morning, the afternoon brought periods of almost unbearable tension, and when Yorkshire were clearly within sight of their object, stony silences alternated with bursts of relief for pent-up feelings.

We have this day seen cricket we shall remember for always, and to-morrow we need to recover our poise. Woolley's batting we know to be above ordinary understanding, and this morning we marvelled, but Sutcliffe brought human ability to the highest possible standard when he won this match for his county. To every man of Kent and Yorkshire, personally successful or disappointed, let all honour and thanks be given, for never have twenty-two cricketers given us greater delight.

An unexpected pleasure and one of deep significance came to those who saw the start of play this morning, for with Ashdown to open the innings went Woolley, and straightaway there was beauty in the air. Woolley and Ashdown had a task clearly before them, and that was to make as many runs as possible in the fleeting minutes during which the wicket slept quiescent beneath the hypnotism of the heavy roller.

The scheme was excellent in theory, but not even Kent's most sanguine supporters could have conceived the perfection of its execution. Woolley, of course, we have long known to be above such mundane considerations as the state of the wicket and the class of the bowling, but Woolley himself has never charmed more magical runs from unwilling opponents than he did in the first unforgettable hour of this morning in June.

Bowes, with Macaulay as his squire, opened the tournament, and quite early in the proceedings he wounded Woolley with a ball that rose quickly and high from the turf and smote the batsman in what is euphemistically known as the 'bread-basket'. Woolley was hurt, and had to rest for a moment, subsequently calling for a drink, but his batting suffered not one whit, for at once he had boundaries, one beyond mid-off, and the other to leg, and within twenty-five minutes there were 32 runs on the board.

Verity in the attack was more helpful to Woolley than to anyone else, and the tempo of the cricket could be adequately judged by the applause that greeted Smailes when he succeeded in bowling two maiden overs to Ashdown.

Neither Smailes nor any other bowler could keep Woolley quiet, of course—Woolley's only quietness lies in the ease of his run-getting, never in the absence of it—and a glorious off drive gave him his sixth 4 and brought his score to 40 for forty minutes' work.

Smailes's proud maidens came tumbling down when Woolley hit him to leg and beyond mid-off, so reaching 50 with but three-quarters of the morning's first hour departed.

Ashdown remembers enough of his early days to know the value of the pull-shot, and this he used to great effect against Verity, so that, with tumultuous cheering for the glory of it all, the 100 was up in very little more than an hour.

Woolley ended on a golden note; he hit Macaulay for 6 to long-on, and was bowled next ball, coming back to the pavilion to a storm of honest clapping that made cricketers of us all.

This fall of the first wicket took place at 12.35, with the total 107; within fifty minutes more Kent were all out for 140. Woolley gone, Macaulay and Verity turned instantly from the innocuous to the demoniac, took every advantage offered by the wicket, now exposed in all its Lamian evil, and became unplayable.

Twice Verity had two wickets in two balls, yet could not manage a 'hat trick', and the biggest stand of any wicket after the first was one of 12 between Todd and Ashdown for the fourth. Everyone except Fagg escaped the indignity of a 'pair', but Chapman and Levett only by the narrowest of margins, and perhaps the outstanding feature of the fifty minutes was a splendidly courageous catch by Sellers, who, at silly mid-off, held a fierce drive from Ashdown.

The 192 runs required must have seemed a monumental total to the Yorkshiremen at lunch, but for every Woolley there is a Leyland (both being equally unique), and he and Sutcliffe began Yorkshire's innings in the same vein as Woolley and Ashdown had played for Kent. For half an hour and more the results were just as happy, for the middle of the bat was used to the ball, and 38 runs were scored, and scored well, before Leyland pulled Freeman with all his might, and Chapman, close in on the leg side, leaned forward and held the bullet within inches of the ground.

Mitchell had his first 4 when he picked out a rank long-hop from Freeman and hooked it fiercely and far; he saw 50 runs made in forty minutes, but at 66 he was leg-before, and Smailes, who followed him, was out first ball.

Smailes was out of luck, for he made his shot bravely and well, and it was only because Fagg was neither at mid-off nor in the long-field, but exercising a roving commission half-way between, that the catch was a catch at all.

This was not to be Barber's match, for at 80, with 3 to his own name, he skied an easy catch to Valentine, and Hutton was leg-before at 91, to make Yorkshire's fifth wicket down.

All this while Sutcliffe was playing irreproachable cricket; never has he picked out more unerringly the ball to be hooked surely and powerfully to the boundary, never has his judgment of what to leave alone been more unfailing, and never can his bat have seemed broader to eager and anxious bowlers. His 50 at twenty-five minutes past three, out of 78 was royally acclaimed, and his shot put up the 100 at five minutes to four.

Wood was his courageous companion for half an hour, during which 29 runs were added, and when he was bowled by Freeman the Yorkshire score was within 72 of the required total.

Upon Wood's fall, at quarter past four, the Kent players proposed tea and made their way towards the pavilion, but Sutcliffe would have none of this irregularity and stayed where he was.   Those fifteen minutes were worth 21 runs to Yorkshire, for Sellers hit two 4's and a grand straight 6, so that at the interval 51 runs were wanted and there were four wickets still to fall.

To settle themselves again after tea both Sutcliffe and Sellers had quick 4's and would have had others but for some magnificent fielding (which, incidentally, has not been the least beautiful part of Kent's cricket all through the match).

Nearer and nearer crept Yorkshire to their haven, quieter and more breathless became the spectators between each ball, so that staccato clapping greeted every run and clapping changed to delirious, hoarse cheering whenever there came a boundary.

At quarter-past five pandemonium broke loose for full five frantic seconds, for at that point Sutcliffe put Wright away to the leg boundary and so completed a century worthy to stand with any in his glorious career.

At 185 bitter blows fell upon Yorkshire, for in two balls Sutcliffe and Verity were out, and an agonizing silence came with Macaulay to the wicket. Within two overs it was finished, Sellers pulling Freeman for 4 to settle the business, and never was boundary more thankfully cheered by frantically-excited spectators.

KENT

First Innings		Second Innings	
Ashdown, b Bowes	8	c Sellers, b Verity	44
Fagg, b Smailes	0	lbw (n), b Macaulay	0
Woolley, lbw, b Macaulay	33	b Macaulay	73
Ames, b Bowes	11	b Macaulay	0
Todd, not out	63	c and b Macaulay	5
B. H. Valentine, st Wood, b Verity	35	c Mitchell, b Verity	3
A. P. F. Chapman, c Bowes, b Macaulay	1	c Macaulay, b Verity	0
W.H.V. Levett, c Sellers, b Verity	0	lbw (n), b Macaulay	1
Wright, st Wood, b Verity	6	st Wood, b Verity	0
Freeman, c and b Verity	6	st Wood, b Verity	7
Lewis, c Sutcliffe, b Leyland	3	not out	0
B. 4, l.b. 10, n.b. 2	16	B. 4, n.b. 3	7
Total	182	Total	140

YORKSHIRE

Sutcliffe, c Woolley, b Freeman	44	lbw, b Freeman	110
Hutton, hit wkt, b Freeman	42	lbw, b Lewis	5
Mitchell, st Ames, b Lewis	1	lbw, b Freeman	10
Leyland, b Lewis	15	c Chapman, b Freeman	15
Barber, lbw, b Freeman	0	c Valentine, b Freeman	3
A.B. Sellers, c Valentine, b Freeman	16	not out	34
Wood, not out	5	b Freeman	11
Verity, lbw, b Freeman	0	b Freeman	0
Smailes, lbw, b Lewis	5	c Fagg, b Freeman	0
Macaulay, st Ames, b Lewis	0	not out	1
Bowes, st Ames, b Freeman	3		
		B. 2, l.b. 1	3
Total	131	Total (for 8 wkts)	192

BOWLING ANALYSIS
KENT
First Innings

	o.	m.	r.	w.			o.	m.	r.	w.
Bowes.	15	2	38	2	Verity .	.	18	4	47	4
Smailes	9	0	36	1	Leyland	.	1	0	1	1
Macaulay	19	6	44	2						

Bowes and Macaulay each bowled a no-ball.

Second Innings

	o.	m.	r.	w.			o.	m.	r.	w.
Bowes.	6	0	28	0	Verity .	.	12·3	1	52	5
Macaulay	12	2	40	5	Smailes	.	3	2	13	0

Macaulay bowled two no-balls and Bowes one no-ball.

YORKSHIRE
First Innings

	o.	m.	r.	w.			o.	m.	r.	w.
Ashdown	5	4	8	0	Freeman	.	23·2	8	47	6
Todd .	3	0	13	0	Lewis .	.	20	6	45	4
Wright	4	0	18	0						

Second Innings

	o.	m.	r.	w.			o.	m.	r.	w.
Freeman	29·1	11	108	7	Todd .	.	3	1	8	0
Lewis	24	7	66	1	Wright	.	2	0	7	0

Umpires : Baldwin and Braund.

THE BEGINNING OF THINGS

WET cricketing days are an abomination and a sore weariness of the flesh, and rarely indeed does any good come from the evil. Fortunate, therefore, do I count myself that an hour of waiting upon one of our county grounds brought me to the acquisition of a little treasure of the game.

It is a paper treasure, bound in paper and labelled most intriguingly; its writer, one H. P.-T., will not be seen again on mortal grounds, but he has left behind him a signal mark of honour to the game he knew and loved so well. His is no epic story of cricket matches lost and won, or cricketers triumphant in their prowess; he has no tale to tell of magic made with bat and ball, but so much did cricket mean to him that he wished to know the whole of it and spent his leisure in constant search for the beginnings of cricket.

Whence did cricket come? Where first did it grow? What was its childhood and what its adolescence? Why are things done as they are done, and what is the significance of this move as opposed to that? These were H. P.-T.'s problems, and in the solving of them he brings to our notice with striking emphasis the ignorance of most of us concerning the game which we believe we know, and which we have all played in one or other of its infinite varieties.

Whence, for example, comes the very name of cricket? There, even H. P.-T. cannot speak with certainty, for there is a mysterious word 'creag' to be explained away in a document dated A.D. 1300 before full acceptance can be accorded to the theory that the game took its title from the curved striking implement used.

That curved nature of the early bat does give us a clue to a cricket term which, at first, seems difficult to understand. Not until we remember that the bat, being no more than a modified tree branch cut or pulled from the trunk, was in its early days similar in shape to the modern hockey stick, do we appreciate the significance of the fieldsman named 'point'; he was 'point' because he stood in the position at which the business end of the bat pointed; and, as the ball was literally bowled and not pitched, 'point' took most of the catches. Thus much have we changed that point to-day is little more than a name, for not one bowler in fifty has a use for this fieldsman.

The other positions in the field are more or less self-explanatory, but there are yet other puzzles which H. P.-T. found occasion to solve. Why are the creases so called? H. P.-T. suggests that when the batsman of early days had taken up his position to defend his single stump (which, of course, was none other than the stump of a tree left standing in some forest clearing), the bowler retired to a suitable distance and there scratched a mark upon the earth. The batsman, in his turn, would allow himself room in which to swing the bat and then, also, scratch a mark for guidance.

As the game developed and wickets were deliberately set up, first at one end and then at both ends, these scratches had of necessity to be more clearly defined, and distinct furrows were made, roughly an inch wide and an inch deep. And here we have our crease, for the old English form of scratch was 'cracche', and from this, or, perhaps, from the French form of 'crevasse', we take our crease.

W. G. Grace mentioned the use of this cut-out crease as within his own early experience, and the whitewashed substitute was apparently adopted in 1865 at the instigation of Alfred Shaw. From this day forward, whenever the umpire remakes the crease with the bail or his toe, I shall remember the beginnings of cricket and H. P.-T.

The umpire himself has a history; he was in old English a 'numpere'—a 'nonpair', called in to settle a dispute between two people. Literally, therefore, there cannot be two 'numperes', but the name remained when the game's growing complications necessitated the service of two men.

The white coat is deliciously accounted for thus:

'The umpire, called in to award decisions, would necessarily have had to know all the ins and outs of the game. As necessarily he would need to have played it. In Cricket's Cradle the odds were 100 to 1 that such a person would be wearing a smock-frock over his ordinary garb. The white-smocked umpire, then, standing among his striplings, divested of their outer garments, like a shepherd among his sheep, would be a customary sight in the country-side playfields. And although the distinctive white coat of the umpire was not adopted in classic cricket until about 1860, one feels sure that it was suggested by such a frequent spectacle. A reminiscence, in fact, like the green cloth of the billiard-table, which is supposed to be a perpetuation of the grassy lawn on which the game was first played."

How well or ill H. P.-T. himself fared in flannels or white smock I do not know, but it is very certain that so great a love as his brought its own reward in one way or another, and if, from his cricket fields elsewhere, he should chance to peep down to earth when the doleful board is being carried around a saturated outfield, 'Look at 4.30,' he may see at least one figure, 'the world forgetting by the world forgot,' challenging the boredom of the raindrops with the pages of H. P.-T.

J. B. HOBBS

HAIL AND FAREWELL, 1934

It is nearly thirty years since John Berry Hobbs, who has now announced his retirement from first-class cricket, played in his first championship match for Surrey; nearly thirty years since he made his first century in first-class cricket; nearly thirty years since he first trod that Oval turf which has known so many of his triumphs. From Hobbs (J. B.), a young man of great promise, he has travelled a long and glorious road to become Jack Hobbs, known the world over and accepted as 'The Master' of cricket. In his springtime cricket was a flourishing flower, full-blown and sweet-o'-scent, for with him on the fields were Trumper and Noble, Maclaren and Jackson, Hirst and Rhodes and a whole host of others whose names are immortal and memories green. Here Hobbs found fortune, for there was stimulating challenge to his genius and knights worthy of his jousting.

No batsman yet seen has evolved such mastery over all the vagaries of bowler and wicket. When the sun shone and runs came merely for the asking, he took them with a thankfulness beyond mere acceptance. He found no pleasure in painstaking effort, in watching the numbers go round; he made every innings a text-book of batting with illustrations entirely his own. A hard Oval wicket meant a good score for Hobbs—that was certain: but how the score would be made was beyond all hope of prophecy. Days were not always thus, for sometimes rain fell and spin bowlers snapped their fingers in glee. Into their hutches the rabbits went tumbling, but Hobbs, amazing the world, remained firm at his end. The pages of cricket reports echo again and again, 'Hobbs played a brilliant innings, where all others failed.' Nor was he a plant of one garden. In every cricketing county of England his magic was seen, and he charmed South Africa and Australia as he charmed the men of his own native land.

When Hobbs first carried his bat for Surrey and for England, bowling strategy was not as in these times. Fast bowlers were fast, scorning swing and relying on speed, length, and break-back. Hobbs mastered these. Medium-paced off-spinners, such as Trumble and Hearne, reaped their harvest of wickets. Hobbs mastered these. Then came the googly with all its attendant alarms. Where others were beaten or hesitant, Hobbs reigned supreme, scoring still with freedom and ease, sure of himself and his power.

The years passed and the fires of Hobbs's youth flared less brightly. A new theory of bowling brought a new batting technique, and nothing in post-War cricket has revealed more grandeur than the autumn of this man's career. From the brilliance of his classical foundation grew the safety and power of his on-side play. No longer was his bat a lance, pennant flying, eagerly routing the foe. The lance became a wand, charming the enemy to impotence and bringing success through calm and assurance. Nothing could have been more beautiful than this later quietening of Hobbs; there were no regrets for the passing of that amazing speed of eye and footwork that were essential to his earlier brilliance.

> " Grow old along with me,
> The best is yet to be."

said Hobbs, and played as Victor Trumper would have played had ever the years grown over him.

Hobbs was never an inhuman, mechanical cricketer; he had a fine sense of duty to the game and its supporters. Runs as represented by marks in the score-book had for him only the value they had to his side. He has thrown away his wicket many times in an attempt to entertain the spectators; he has got himself out as though saying, 'You must be tired of me now.' His records, the bare framework to his picture, are in themselves a source of wonder. He has passed the century 197 times; over 61,000 runs has he made in the aggregate; 323 runs he shared with Wilfred Rhodes for a first-wicket partnership in Test cricket. On sixteen occasions in one season he made a score of more than 100. Is it credible that any one man will ever do more?

Yet not for these things alone, or even mainly, will he be beloved in our memory. We shall think of him, trim and tidy, coming out to open the innings; we shall see the twirling of the bat before each ball, the easy, perfectly-poised stance at the wicket, those dancing feet move swiftly back or forward, and we shall dream of him 'burning the grass with boundaries', his bat flashing forth every stroke known to cricket. With Grace and Trumper and Ranji he stands incomparable—our debt is beyond all hope of payment.

WORCESTER AND WORCESTERSHIRE

WORCESTER is no place for hurried or discontented entry, for it is by no means the least handsome of our older cities. Its chief glory lies in a cathedral that stands commandingly upon the river bank and watches with unceasing patience the Western entrance to the town.

The atmosphere of cathedrals the world over has a similarity of majesty and calm, and in the mighty monument of Worcester there is no lack of these abiding qualities; in addition there is an air of brightness, almost of urbanity, that strikes you immediately you enter the doors. You never feel yourself on sufferance in Worcester Cathedral; you are welcomed no less by the stones and mortar and stained glass than by the helpful mortals who will show you all you thought to see and point out beauties that your ignorance might have overlooked.

Worcester has not perhaps the awesome impressiveness of York Minster or the cold solemnity of Peterborough, but there is spaciousness and dignity to mingle with the friendliness. Within its walls lie the tombs of John, the least beloved of our kings, and that Prince Arthur who, had he lived to keep the eighth Henry from the throne, might well have changed the course of history.

It is said of John that deathbed qualms impelled him to give orders for his body to be wrapped in monkish gown and hood, that so disguised he might slip past the gates of paradise, and it is certainly on record that when his coffin was opened the bones were covered with what seemed to be the remnants of monastic garb. Poor John! I doubt if his faults were greater than his misfortunes, for his principal failing was weakness in an age that revered little but strength. How many of us could hope to leave a better story were our lot cast in high places with contemporaries and posterity agog to judge our every action and the fate of a nation depending upon our word.

Should you be strong and of good courage you may climb the tower of Worcester Cathedral, through the rafters, past the belfry, winding upwards and upwards until you come to a view of half the west of England. Strength is needed because the climb is long and the stairway steep, courage because if the bells ring out when you are near the belfry there comes the shock of a world changed without warning into a chaos of noise and mighty shudderings.

From the roof of the tower you look across the river to the county cricket ground. Here indeed is beauty, though sometimes it is beauty hid beneath the waters for there are marks upon a post of the pavilion to show the various levels of the floods.

Sometimes a tree is pointed out to strangers as being the one among whose topmost branches the heavy roller was found after an inundation, but this story, I feel, has less authority behind it than that which tells of a visiting cricketer who swam from the pavilion to the wickets some years ago.

We were walking down to the Worcester ground one morning when Michael paused to gaze across the parapet of the bridge upon the quiet water of the river. I asked him what he sought, and he told me of the days when the transmission of evening paper messages was not so simple as it is now. A journalist of wide repute was spending a particularly busy afternoon in the press-box and sending his 'copy' by an aged messenger into the city, there to be dealt with. No sooner was one message sent off from the ground than the preparation of another had to be begun, and there was little leisure for the writer. Judge, therefore, of his emotion when his Mercury returned some few minutes after one departure and announced to an unkindly joyous multitude: 'Write some more papers, mister; wind's blown them other across the bridge into the river!'

The byways of Worcester will afford entertainment as long as you care to roam them, but just as Worcester's grace is not all contained in the Cathedral so Worcestershire has more to offer than her county town. Every mile of the shire is a traveller's delight, and if Kent be the garden of

England, surely Worcestershire is the country estate.

Within ten miles of Worcester city lie the Malvern townships sheltering beneath hills as geologically ancient as any in the land. You may climb these ancient rocks by wandering paths and steep, and should fortune be with you your reward is ample, for away to the south-west Brecon and the Bristol Channel are visible, east lies mile upon mile of the English plain, and the western horizon is broken and ragged with the mountains of Wales. Can any one spot give a view quite comparable to this which may be seen from the remains of that British camp which was a township before ever the Romans crossed the Channel?

Between Worcester and Birmingham sits the spa of Droitwich with surely the most remarkable baths in the world. Here the water is so saturated with brine that it is quite impossible for the bather to sink. It is common practice to lie on the water reading a newspaper or taking tea pushed out on a tray by the attendant. As a tonic, this bath stands supreme, as a sensation it must be experienced to be believed.

Droitwich is henceforth a calling place for Michael and me whenever we are near its charming valley with an hour to call our own.

YORKSHIRE PUDDING

YORKSHIRE County cricket does not begin upon the fields of Bradford, Leeds, or Sheffield any more than a meal begins with the placing of the dishes before the diner. Behind the appearance of those dishes lies care and forethought and organization in the kitchens, and behind that there must be enthusiasm and inspiration. So to make possible these games of bat and ball which are so dear to us, there are months and years of toil, of trial and error, and whole generations of enthusiasm.

Yorkshire cricket begins upon those fields bare of grass and innocent of any amenity save space, where boys with broken bats and shapeless balls imitate their heroes of another sphere. There was a time when almost every Yorkshire village could show you a cricket match in the street during the dinner hour of the factories and workshops. Then boys and men would forget the morning's cares and the worries of the afternoon in play, and cricket was always the game. Men who played in good club cricket every Saturday would not scorn this elementary practice and boys would treasure for weeks together the memory of an envied wicket taken or a good run scored. By-laws and motor buses have removed most of this cricket to-day, but the spirit remains and seeks outlet elsewhere, with the old ambition unquenched and the old joys merely transferred to another scene.

Almost always the young Yorkshire boy has the county eleven upon the limit of his horizon. With his dream an ever-present companion, he plays for the nearest available team. From school he goes to his church, from church to the second eleven of some prominent club; further promotion brings him into the first team and important league cricket, and watchful eyes note his progress and bring him to the attention of the county authorities. Winter nets, spring coaching, success in the Colts, and the end of a journey is at hand, and another cricketer wears the beloved White Rose upon his cap.

Few counties achieve success without the backbone of good club cricket, and Yorkshire is particularly fortunate, if inevitably so, in the excellence of the leagues that provide entertainment and recreation for thousands of people each Saturday of summer. There club cricket has tremendous strength and force, and is in itself an ideal as well as a stepping stone to higher things. Far more cricketers remain league players than ever go beyond, but few indeed are the men to represent Yorkshire who do not pass through this training ground. Indeed, there are cases of Yorkshiremen qualifying for other counties who are sent back to their Yorkshire league each Saturday for the best possible experience during the period of waiting.

Sometimes the training course in the league is long and anxious, and of late years, in particular, players have been drafted into the Yorkshire side at a greater age than is customary in the cricketer setting out to make a name for himself with his county. Sometimes a young player comes within the county's sphere of activities without having had league experience; invariably he is then allocated to a league club and his performances there watched and analysed. It is of enormous significance that of the present Yorkshire team, Sellers, Sutcliffe, Barber, Wood, and Hutton played in the Bradford League, and Leyland, Verity, Turner, and Smailes have had experience in the Yorkshire Council.

This league cricket is a testing ground for both the technique and temperament of a young cricketer. Here a man learns the difference between playing for amusement and playing for a purpose; his mental cricket is developed in an atmosphere to which carelessness or indolence are entirely foreign and where the light excuse of 'It's only a game' is scornfully rejected. League cricket is not merely a game; it is a business in the form of a game, and none the less pleasant for the seriousness and responsibility involved, for the greater the earnestness and endeavour demanded the sweeter the taste of success when it comes.

In league cricket the player learns that there are no inconsequent moments and comes to realize that his every action is observed and has meaning. He learns that continual care and concentration alone can bring success, for where the standard is high any defection must of necessity prove fatal. As a batsman he meets professional bowlers who know all there is to be known of guile and cunning and who exhibit invariably the cardinal virtue of length; thus he comes to curb his natural impatience and grows selective in his moments of attack. As a bowler he meets batsmen who rarely fail to take advantage of opportunities and who must be thought as well as bowled out; thus he appreciates the necessity of bowling to his field, and adapting himself to the needs of a particular situation.

Where championships and cups are at stake and matches watched by distinctly partisan spectators, tense situations arise, and until the young player has been tested in the nerve-racking fires of close finishes and knotty problems, he cannot account himself in any way experienced. The light of publicity is upon him as a league player, he learns calm philosophy when all his world knows of his failures and acquires self-control in times of elation.

From all this it might appear that Yorkshire league cricket is a very grim and forbidding experience, but, in actual fact, it is nothing of the kind, for the lessons are mainly self-taught and follow so inevitably in the course of playing that the learning is chiefly subconscious, and only the sense of responsibility differentiates league cricket from any other kind of club cricket. Yorkshire cricket may have a pronouncedly business-like air, but that is because the Yorkshireman has business-like qualities and prefers his life, even his sporting life, to be run on that principle.

With a few seasons of league cricket behind him, a player has very sound technique and spiritual qualifications for the county game and requires only polish and experience to make him a first-class product. It would be idle to pretend that league cricket and first-class cricket differ only in the time element, for there is much to be learned by the county cricketer that never comes within the sphere of the club player; yet, in fundamentals, the game is the same, and it is surely beyond argument that the league cricketer has a considerable advantage over his colleague whose training has been less arduous, when the time comes for the strain and fierce light of county cricket.

When a Yorkshire cricketer has attained county status, he becomes at once part of a tradition that he has known and appreciated all his life. Consciously or unconsciously, he realizes that he is treading in the footsteps of great predecessors and that there is a noble heritage in his keeping. He knows also that the eyes of the county are upon him and his doings; not cast carelessly in his direction

in idle moments of leisure; but following him everywhere and appreciating success or demanding
explanation of failure. A Yorkshire cricketer is not
responsible only to his captain and committee for
the charge in his keeping; he is responsible to fellow
cricketers all over the county and that responsibility
colours his existence and stiffens his determination
to deserve well of his friends, known and unknown.

The huge and envied membership of the Yorkshire County Cricket Club comes not only from the
appreciation of value for one guinea, but from the
earnest belief among Yorkshiremen that the county's
cricket must receive adequate and enthusiastic support. It is a point of honour with followers to see as
much cricket as possible, not only because there is
pleasure to be had, but also because it is a matter
of personal importance to watch over the county's
cricket representatives.

Apart from the general interest in the team as a
whole, each district of Yorkshire has a personal
interest in its particular contributions to the side.
Sheffield rejoices at Turner's success; Bradford has
a particularly warm welcome for Wood; all Pudsey
knows Sutcliffe and Hutton as its own sons. This
interest never flags in good years or bad, and
Yorkshire's players, knowing this, find an added
incentive to improvement which goes beyond
personal considerations.

Great as have been Yorkshire's cricketers as

individuals, it is as a team that the county has won
most lasting renown, and it is because of the realization by each player of his personal responsibility
to his colleagues and to his county as a whole that
the team-work has attained so high a standard.
Yorkshire cricket, on the field and off, is run
primarily as a business (certainly as a pleasurable
business), and in business little progress can be
made without co-operation. To watch a Yorkshire
eleven in the field is to find living illustration of
cricket co-operation; there is no confused wandering
of fieldsmen when a bowling change is made, no
hovering in doubtful positions when this or that
bowler is at work. Rarely indeed does the Yorkshire
attack seem to be at its wits' end; rarely indeed is the
side put to rout even in the fiercest blaze of batsmanship. So, too, in batting, one Yorkshireman knows
how to make himself subservient to another for the
good of his side. Is it not conceivable that Mitchell
may have made an even greater personal name under
another banner?   Yet Mitchell is in the truest
tradition of Yorkshire cricketers, placing always side
before self and working always to the common,
rather than the individual good.

It is not by accident that Yorkshire has achieved
enviable success in the County Championship. It is
through long hours of quiet and unassuming work,
persistence here, inspiration there, and a perpetual
consciousness of a tradition to keep. So long as

Yorkshiremen in general preserve their characteristics of earnestness and enthusiasm and a full realization that the whole is greater than the part, with the object utterly and incontestably worth the striving, so long will Yorkshire cricket maintain the standard that has brought the admiration of the cricketing world.

HERBERT SUTCLIFFE

IT is a common cry that modern cricket lacks such personalities as graced it in the 'Golden Age' when every county had one man or more who attracted the crowds as much by himself as by his performances.

It is unfortunately true that one innings has become very like another innings and one white figure in the field could easily be mistaken for another white figure. At most first-class matches to-day a scorecard is an absolute necessity, for even bowling methods have become abominably stereotyped.

There are still, however, one or two figures whom none could fail to recognize. Herbert Sutcliffe is unquestionably one of them. When he stands in the field his shining black hair and immaculate flannels serve as clear identification, and when he is at the wicket his presence is unmistakable.

Sutcliffe holds so many records that he who knows not this player's reputation knows nothing of cricket. To watch one of Sutcliffe's innings is to have complete understanding of his power. He always seems to me rather to hurry to the wicket, everlastingly anxious to be batting and eager to test the quality of a bat which looks brand-new every time he opens an innings. Nine times out of ten the first ball will be outside the off-stump, and just so often will Sutcliffe step across, bring his feet together with military precision, lift that beautiful bat high out of harm's way and gaze past point as the ball thuds into the wicket-keeper's gloves.

This padding-up announces as clearly as spoken words: 'My dear bowler, you are wasting your time: I am proposing to make a century to-day and I am certainly not going to jeopardize my chances by feeling for anything outside the off-stump.' The bowler is invariably heedless, but when Sutcliffe performs precisely the same operation at half-past five in the afternoon scepticism begins to depart.

Sutcliffe's appearance is, of course, in keeping with his character. He looks cool and calm, and he behaves coolly and calmly. The bowler who beats Sutcliffe's bat and misses the stumps by a 'coat of varnish' may save himself the trouble of throwing up his arms and calling upon high heaven to witness the luck of the man. Sutcliffe will be quite unimpressed by such display. In all probability he will not even turn round to assure himself that the bails are still on. I have seen Sutcliffe beaten and morally bowled three times in six balls, yet at the end of the over he stood aside, leaned on his bat and crossed his legs in exactly the same way as when there are 200 chanceless runs to his name.

To be morally out is a conception beyond Sutcliffe's ken when applied to himself, and of all cricketers he is the most unlikely to end his innings through worry.

When a man of this temperament adds to his accomplishments a wonderful technique, he is obviously approaching the ideal for the stress and strain of Test match cricket. The certainty of Sutcliffe's defence, the power of his hooking and driving, and the accuracy of his placing would probably have brought him many runs for England in any circumstances. But without the alliance of those inward qualities which make him never happier than when difficulties abound and the situation calls for almost superhuman effort he could not have astonished the world as he has done.

Sutcliffe's records and runs are dear to his fellow Yorkshiremen, who recognize and respect high ability; his physical strength and his patience through the hottest of cricketing days are admired because Yorkshiremen envy and honour a man's man; his willingness to enter the struggle and his success with everything against him are the real keys to his great popularity, because Yorkshiremen and cricketers everywhere dearly love a fighter.

Not only along the ways of county cricket has Sutcliffe marched triumphantly; equal success has come to him in Test matches, and his work for England, at home and abroad, has been a source of wonder and envy the world over. Many of Sutcliffe's efforts for England have been made in adverse circumstances, for he and Hobbs had invariably great responsibilities in the way of big scores against them or difficult batting conditions. How they triumphed is a matter of history, and no cricketer can read without pride of the gallant deeds of defiance inspired by the inherent greatness of these players. Sutcliffe has given a great deal to cricket. On the field he has built upon the foundations of those who went before and himself added a superstructure that is at once beautiful and inspiring. Always he has played the game as it should be played, in high courage and sporting endeavour, and given of his best at all times. Off the field, he has set himself an equally high standard, and no action of his has ever reflected other than creditably upon his profession.

A HAT IN A HUNDRED

Leicester, *August*, 1935.

HERBERT SUTCLIFFE is a great batsman. He is more than that; he is a great personality and is himself under any guise or disguise. To-day he played a double century innings for Yorkshire, watching the ball for most of the time from beneath the brim of a grey trilby hat, and although he is perfectly entitled to wear a trilby hat or a top hat or a pitman's cap should he so desire, it is doubtful if any one other than Sutcliffe in present-day cricket could have appeared thus without provoking audible comment from the crowd.

With or without hat Sutcliffe was a very fine batsman to-day, and he not only laid the foundation of Yorkshire's score but remained at the wicket to do a good deal of decorative work. Once or twice he had disturbed moments when the ball did not behave as expected upon pitching, but for the most part he was a superbly serene Sutcliffe, watching and waiting the arrival of half volleys and full tosses which meant boundaries as surely as they came.

It is generally accepted that he is not a great batsman who must needs wait for his runs to come from bowling deficiencies, but the day's object for Sutcliffe consisted of more than mere run-getting for himself. He might perhaps have made a quick

50 and seen the rest of the day's play from a shady seat, but he preferred to induce in the Leicestershire bowlers that state of mind which looks upon the taking of wickets as something to be read about in history books and the only rests from toil being the intervals of custom—at lunch and tea. That Leicestershire never quite reached this stage was scarcely Sutcliffe's fault, and if wickets did fall it was only at long and irregular intervals and there were many Yorkshire runs in between.

The day's beginning was all Sutcliffe, for that batsman had early 4's with a leg hit from a no-ball and a late cut, whilst Hutton spent twenty minutes in thinking things over before scoring his first run of the morning. Sutcliffe himself always put comfort before speed, but he left Hutton far behind, and a perfectly placed shot through the covers made him 36 to Hutton's 12 and the total 52 at twenty-five minutes past twelve.

Sutcliffe took off his hat for the first time just before one o'clock to acknowledge the applause in appreciation of his 50, but in this same over the first wicket partnership ended at 79 when Hutton was lbw. to Marlow. Hutton, so far as I remember, never made a false shot, but he could do no more than put the ball to the fieldsman, and whatever the bowlers may have thought about him, the spectators were clearly disappointed.

Sutcliffe, too, had a critic in the stand who gave

advice and expression of opinion in anything but a modest whisper. But what effect could one poor voice be expected to have upon a man who has triumphed over the commentary of the 'Hill' at Sydney. Sutcliffe looked once in the direction of the offender and turned back to the game to put up the 100 in two and a quarter hours and swing a full toss negligently to the leg boundary.

Coincidence came into the cricket at lunch-time. Then Yorkshire had collected exactly as many runs as did Leicestershire yesterday, and a wicket again fell to the last ball of the morning, this time Mitchell being bowled when he hit over a ball pitched well up.

Barber brought a fresh mind and body to the treatment of the bowling after lunch, and at once pulled Prentice for 4. He was unceremonious and unrepentant, and hit boundaries with or without provocation.

To a certain extent he stimulated Sutcliffe, who, however, was never prepared to forget his dignity in any riotous or ill-manned swinging of the bat, and more than 70 Yorkshire runs came in an hour. Just before three o'clock Sutcliffe reached his hundred out of 172, and promptly put on his hat which had been neglected since lunch, thus stating clearly as though in written words that one hundred was merely a beginning to the day's labours.

At 3.25 Yorkshire were 200 and the welcome new ball immediately gave Leicestershire a wicket when

Barber was caught low down in the gully. A shower of rain gave everyone rest and peace for a quarter of an hour, but the interruption made little difference to Turner and none at all to Sutcliffe, so that Leicestershire had to wait 81 runs before further success came their way and Turner was beautifully caught low down at second slip.

Wood must see another day before his season's thousand runs can come to him, for wanting 20 he had made 11 when he tried to cut Astill and became a picture of amazed dismay as the ball turned back and bowled him. Even Sutcliffe, guardian of Yorkshire's fortunes, smiled. There was no alarm at the comparatively quick fall of this wicket, for Yorkshire were by this time 321 and three-quarters of an hour remained for easy runs to be taken from a tired attack.

It is not altogether to the batsmen's credit that this tired bowling was allowed to keep a length and demand defensive forward strokes. Surely this was the time for number seven on the list to break pavilion windows or perish in the attempt; surely five wickets left justified the possible risk in the long field, but all was quiet and careful until at ten minutes past six Sutcliffe became 200.

When any batsman makes 200 the day must be accounted solely his, and in every way Sutcliffe was Yorkshire on this Thursday of August. Whether or not his work will bring victory remains to be seen, but the glory of the achievement remains independent of the result, and not the least remarkable feature of the accomplishment lay in the fact that he was running short singles as well in the day's last minutes as in the morning hours.

Ten minutes from the close Sellers was caught from a mishit to cover, and the players left the field with Yorkshire 109 runs ahead and Sutcliffe (hatless) not out 210.

LEICESTERSHIRE
First Innings

Shipman, b Fisher	8
Berry, b Fisher	13
Armstrong, lbw, b Rawlin . . .	38
Watson, c Sellers, b Rawlin . . .	58
Prentice, c Turner, b Rawlin . . .	41
N. Dowan, lbw, b Fisher . . .	40
Coleman, c Turner, b Verity . . .	0
Astill, c Turner, b Verity . . .	0
Corrall, not out	38
Marlow, b Bowes	6
Smith, b Verity	25
B. 5, l.b. 2	7
	—
Total	274

YORKSHIRE
First Innings

Sutcliffe, not out	210
Hutton, lbw (n), b Marlow . . .	18
Mitchell, b Prentice . . .	10
Barber, c Smith, b Shipman . . .	41
Turner, c Smith, b Astill . . .	33
Wood, b Astill	11
A. B. Sellers, c Smith, b Astill . . .	33
Verity, not out	2
B. 10, l.b. 12, w. 3 . . .	25
	—
Total (for 6 wkts) . . .	383

Fisher, Bowes, and Rawlin to bat.

Bowling Analysis

Leicestershire
First Innings

	o.	m.	r.	w.		o.	m.	r.	w.
Bowes	23	2	66	1	Verity	31	13	80	3
Rawlin	18	3	43	3	Turner	4	0	11	0
Fisher	29	7	67	3					

Umpires : Hardstaff and Dipper.

MAURICE LEYLAND

MODERN cricket is supposed to be lacking in outstanding personalities, but without delving into the
pros and cons of that particular question there can
be little doubt that Maurice Leyland, player for his
county and country, is a cricketing character who
would not have been negligible in any age. He is
a sufficiently good cricketer to be an early choice
for the England team but, as with all the really
great, it is the man who interests us even more than
his deeds. Leyland will be clearly remembered
when the pages recording his runs are time-stained
and torn.

He is a direct descendant in spirit of George Hirst
and Roy Kilner. In him the crowd has a friend, one
who suffers as they do from the boredom of safety-
first batting and unimaginative bowling, and he does
his best to relieve us of either. No one ever called
Leyland dull. There have been occasions when he
could not or would not score quickly, but behind
the defence one could almost see his hands itching
to swing his bat freely in a search for the thrill of a
six. That he could restrain himself in such circumstances is a tribute to his cricketing honour; the
call of side before self, however personally irksome,
never found Leyland unheeding. But his natural

style is all quest for adventure, and no man playing to-day can hit the ball harder.

There have been, and no doubt there will be, in cricket better left-hand bats than this man. Woolley, for example, is more perfect in his stroke production. Clem Hill, more sound in defence, and Warren Bardsley and Hampshire's Mead spring readily to mind. Leyland's footwork is not without fault, and we can see him any day cracking boundaries in something far from the classical mode. We have seen him caught at cover point from scandalously bad shots, and we have seen him 'feeling' for balls on the off-side in a manner no well-coached school-boy would countenance.

But Leyland has something more than the rule book for his shots. He has a wonderful eye which makes the timing of the ball easy to him, and a pair of strong forearms which give almost unbelievable power to his shots. Not that the straight bat and the classical tradition are unknown to him. Put him in a Test Match with instructions that the game must be saved, and then watch his method. No feet were ever more accurately in position, no bat held straighter, and no technique more fundamentally sound than his then. There is an excellent batsman, but one who is a cog in the England machine, not Maurice Leyland the individual man, though it is part of his greatness that he can and does sink his own personality, his own heartfelt desires, and play for his side to the last bitter hour when necessity drives.

Of his international cricket an epic story could be written, for there are very few batting glories that have not been his. In his first match against Australia he made a hundred, and rare the occasion when he has not 'come off', leading some desperate rearguard action, or crowding on all sail to drive home an advantage. In recent series he has been England's outstanding batsman, ever reliable, fearless, and strong.

But it is not in Test cricket that I like to think of Leyland. I picture him rather where the sunshine is gracious, and the ultimate result not hovering always; on some field where he can swing his free bat with no care in the world, and the joy of the game simply bubbling from his every happy movement; where his bat is a sword cutting and carving delicious, magical strokes, enchanting opponents, spectators, and all, with the sunniest smile on his broad, pleasant face, himself the personification of everything good in a Yorkshireman.

Leyland is no niggard in his gifts. He opens his store and shows us his all; cuts, glances, hooks, drives, you may see some of each in one innings in quick, surprising succession, and to his opponents he is the most generous and knightly of men. Not for him the long drawn-out agony of quarterless struggle and infinite labour; not for him the amassing of records of mountainous scores.

His challenge is there for his enemies to see, and he never retires behind an impregnable armour of caution and 'safety-first' to try tempers and drive hearts to ultimate bitterness and scorn. 'Bowl me the ball,' he appears to be saying, 'If I can hit it, I will; if you bowl me out—well, the sun will still shine and to-morrow I will joust with you again.'

A very great compliment was once paid to Leyland, though as far as I know he himself never received it. 'I will leave the bar any time to watch Leyland batting,' it was said, and this was no wordy sacrifice, but a genuine renunciation of one pleasure for another.

For myself I also find pleasure when Leyland is fielding; even there the man's individuality stands out to rival his skill. Happiest in the outfield, no hope of a save is too forlorn for him to neglect, no effort too great for him to consider the striving not worth while. He has particularly safe hands, and cool, confident judgment, and his little skip before his left-handed throw is redolent with physical fitness and energy.

Even all this takes no account of his bowling, but in all probability Leyland himself takes very little account of that. His bowling is a thing of monstrous and fanciful spin, seaside holiday bowling where a spade is the bat and the wicket a stanchion of the pier.

How Leyland must laugh when he takes a wicket; how great a joke he considers the whole thing to be.

At Bradford he once took two wickets in two successive balls, deliveries as bad as deliveries well could
be, and as the third batsman walked in, Leyland
hurried half-way back to the pavilion wall to make
his mark while the crowd roared with merriment.

That, of course, is why we like him so much. He is
never aloof from us, never coldly superior, and grim
the day indeed when he fails to give us a smile.

THE THOUGHTFUL STUDENT

VERY rarely in its history has cricket known so persistently thoughtful a student as Hedley Verity, of Yorkshire and England. C. B. Fry was perhaps the batsman complementary to this bowler, but not even Fry, whose study reduced batsmanship almost to scientific formulae, gave his attention more wholeheartedly to the game than does Verity.

Rumour credits Verity with planning destruction for batsmen in the course of his morning shave, and cloaks him with an aura of cricket that surrounds him in eating, sleeping, and all conversation. Rumour, no doubt, exaggerates, but of Verity's deep study of cricket there can be no manner of doubt.

There was a time, or so it seemed, when this absorption threatened to become as manifest a fault as in the ordinary way it is a virtue, for there have been occasions when Verity became 'sickled o'er with the pale cast of thought', and spent so much time in laying plans to deceive his enemies that he neglected to use the weapons the gods had given him, and ignored spin upon turning wickets to engage in the less obvious delights of a battle of wits.

To 'think' men out when you are without allies and in unhelpful circumstances is admirable devotion to duty, but to waste opportunities in experiment when the wicket cries aloud for nothing other than length and spin is to ride in the face of fortune.

It always seemed to me that Verity took some time to recover from the effects of that unique plan of campaign pursued by Jardine's team in Australia. There it was Verity's task to hold the enemy in a state of as near as possible to stagnation whilst England's principal attacking forces were regathering strength. Verity came back to our county cricket with what I can only describe (and with much reluctance, for the phrase is far from beautiful) as a 'maiden-complex'. He seemed content with negative success and appeared satisfied to permit batsmen to stay at the crease providing they acknowledged themselves under his control.

This characteristic proved, happily, but a phase, and there is now no bowler in the world more to be feared when the ball will turn. The benevolent despot has become the insistent conqueror.

In this mood Verity is a great bowler indeed. Many times has he been declared the natural successor to Peel and Wilfred Rhodes, but here, I fancy, less than justice is being done to Verity and to those who went before. Verity is not quite in the true line of slow left-arm spin bowlers.

With Rhodes there went a sense of peace and inevitability that I, at least, cannot experience with Verity. Rhodes from the ringside you knew as

perfection almost to the extent of monotony. Not for
the spectator's sight was that delicate variation of pace
and of length; for him there was only the same sweet
action, the same smooth curve of flight, and the per-
sistent drop-drop-drop upon the batsman's doorstep.
You knew Rhodes would get his wicket; when the
ball would turn, it did turn, and the fall was expected
every minute; when the wicket was good, patience
was necessary, but the result was only delayed, always
forthcoming sooner or later. A man cannot take considerably more than 3,000 wickets for Yorkshire alone
by waiting for turf that favours him. Unless you
were batting against him you could only appreciate
the true genius of Rhodes in retrospect. It all seemed
so simple at the time.

Verity has less delicacy. His antagonism is much
more marked. He is faster through the air than was
Rhodes and by virtue of his height he gets higher
from the pitch. Indeed, it is not upon the truly sticky
wicket that Verity is at his most deadly; he has nothing like the finger spin of Colin Blythe, and he is perhaps most potent when the ball 'stands up' rather
than turns quickly. So it was at Lord's on that
memorable Test Match day in 1934.

Verity's menace you can see and share from the
spectator's seat. You can appreciate the fact that the
ball leaves his hand with some imp of evil in it; Verity
himself announces it as he stoops forward at the end
of his follow through or throws up an expectant arm

as the batsman plunges blindly to the approximate pitch.

Verity upon a day of success is the personification of hostility. A batsman fallen a victim to him might return to the pavilion assuring himself: 'Couldn't help it; it's quite impossible to play the man to-day.' In the bowling of Rhodes there was greater allurement, and the batsman was rarely left satisfied; then he thought, as he walked the long, lone walk, 'I am an ass; I'm quite sure I need not have got out to that ball—I wonder what I did wrong.' For thirty years the world's greatest batsmen kept wondering what they had done wrong, and I do not suppose they ever solved the problem.

Verity's attack has one feature that is very rarely found in the equipment of slow bowlers: his faster ball, beautifully hidden until the last half of his arm's swing, comes down at considerably above medium pace. Here, of course, his physical attributes help him, for his height makes it unnecessary for him to toss the ball up, and perhaps more than anyone, save Colin Blythe, Verity gets results from this fast ball. Even to the suspicious it is dangerous, because of the really remarkable change of pace.

How much Verity owes to his fieldsmen is quite beyond calculation. It is idle to say that had he played for any county other than Yorkshire his success would have been materially lessened, for who knows but that Verity's bowling would have developed fieldsmen elsewhere?

As it is, we can say that if ever Verity goes into business and requires assistance, no partnership would be more appropriate or familiar in sound than that of 'Mitchell and Verity'. The number of astonishing catches Mitchell has taken for Verity is legion, and the fieldsman's anticipation is now so remarkable that times beyond counting we see him darting from the gully to the bat's edge even as the ball is pitching. This is fielding to perfection, and Verity must be uncommonly grateful to have it at his disposal.

FUN AND FROLIC

Twice within the last week or so I have had cause for real merriment upon a cricket field, and it is not without significance that in each case the humorist was Leyland and the setting Lord's.

The significance lies, of course, in the fact that Leyland is one of the very few merry—merry, as distinct from contented or complacent—cricketers now before us, and his enjoyment is in no way marred by self-consciousness even amongst the dignity of cricket's headquarters.

Leyland's bowling is mostly a joke, but sometimes it is an extremely practical joke, and there was more than one reason beneath the delight when a slow full-toss descended from a seemingly mountainous height and bowled one of the Middlesex batsmen, who had retreated, for some reason best known to himself, far in the direction of square leg. No sooner had the ball hit the stumps than Leyland snatched off his cap and threw it gleefully on high. He was pleased, he was amused, and his pleasure and his amusement extended all round the ground. That is personality.

Later in the week some member of the opposing side was bowled, monumentally bowled with two stumps laid flat upon the earth; the third reeled pathetically, and Leyland, who was not the bowler,

strolled across the pitch and plucked the remaining
stump from its socket to throw it with its companions.
'Let's do the thing properly,' his action said.

Perhaps I am easily amused that these trivial incidents should remain in my mind and be remembered
with so much pleasure. Be that as it may. I am
nevertheless grateful to Leyland for the humour of
these moments. Too often am I left without a smile
in the day's cricket; too often do I have the feeling
that there is lack of humanity in to-day's cricket and
to-day's cricketers. I am the last person to encourage
or condone buffoonery in cricket; the game is one of
infinite dignity and poise, it is a serious game to be
played in all seriousness or not at all, but there is flesh
and blood in cricket, too, and laughter is the privilege
of humanity.

Cricket has always had its humorists of one kind or
another and has always been the better for their presence. Perhaps most notable of all was Lancashire's
Parkin, a man who almost buried his technical excel-
lences beneath a host of quips and cranks and wanton
wiles. Indeed I am inclined to believe that mention of
Parkin's name would call to mind his famous conjur-
ing trick before it brought up visions of his lovely,
flowing action and his ceaseless, brilliant experiment.

Parkin bowled as very few bowlers before or since
have bowled; the whole art of spin and strategy was at
his command and many were his deeds and wonderful. For this he was appreciated by the crowds, but

appreciation was turned to real and rare affection when he thrust out a foot to induce the rolling ball to jump into his waiting hand. Many, many times has this trick been done, and done successfully, since Parkin's day, but the imitation has never been complete. None other has had quite Parkin's nonchalance or air of 'Oh, it's easy!' To anyone who knew Parkin as a cricketer it will be no surprise to learn that he was also a card manipulator and conjuror of considerable repute.

Parkin's humours did not rest with this one feature. Whenever he got to the wicket, bat in hand, there was entertainment without pause. He was no batsman comic in incompetence; he could make runs or support a rearguard action when necessity arose, but the imp within him was usually irrepressible. He would chase up and down the wicket with unflagging energy, taunting flurried fieldsmen to run him out if they could. Conservative computation puts half Parkin's total runs down to overthrows. The most sober and self-assured of sides have been lured into scrambling confusion by Parkin's antics.

'Though this were madness, there were method in't,' and Lancashire foolery has often brought Lancashire profit. When Parkin left first-class cricket he left a gap that has not yet been filled. It was his pleasure that our edification should also be our entertainment, and joyously we bade him welcome and with sorrow saw him go.

To-day's jesters are few and scarcely of Parkin's calibre, but whilst Hendren remains cricket will not be without smiles. Hendren's fun is both verbal and practical. When he fields upon the boundary edge he will share his wit with near-by spectators; for this he was beloved of Australians who, for all their faults, are as ready to laugh at themselves as at anyone else.

Hendren it was who returned an apple from the outfield to the vast surprise of a wicket-keeper expecting the ball. Hendren it was who put a noted fast bowler completely out of his stride in his run-up by the sudden projection of an ample posterior and the assumption of an alarming facial expression.

Hendren is a great batsman who has seen his county and his country through many trying times, but never has failure or defeat robbed him of his sportsmanship or his sense of humour. Hendren must be more precious than gold to the organizers of cricket festivals, for it is his nature to

" Mix with kings, nor lose the common touch."

And it is the common touch that is the charm of Hendren and of all humorists.

THE CHARM OF LORD'S

FEW of us like idle hours upon a cricket field, and particularly unhappy are those enforced by rain and unkind weather; but sometimes a ground itself has attractions that are independent of the cricket that is being played, or should be played, within its boundaries. Only the familiarity of the longest of acquaintanceships could make Lord's dull, for instance, cricket match or no cricket match.

Lord's stands alone as a home of the game. No other habitation of cricketers is quite like it; some may be more pretentious, some more luxurious, some have greater beauty of setting, but none has superior attraction to this, the most famous cricket ground the world knows.

Chief amongst the charming characteristics of Lord's is its dignity. This you feel even outside the walls in St. John's Wood Road; to arrive breathless and dishevelled at the main gate would be an offence almost beyond forgiveness, and would certainly spoil your appreciation of the day's play.

Once I recommended an Australian visitor to go to Lord's and immediately he referred to it as 'the place where you take your hat off as you go in'. No gesture could be more appropriate, for Lord's does command respect, and, in return, it has

to offer the most delectable prospect cricketers
can know.

Few other places so happily mingle formality and
comfort. Not only are you permitted to walk upon
historic turf, but ritual bids you do so at each and
every interval. Tradition lingers without dispute even
in this casual age; there are seats where smoking is
forbidden; there are portions strictly reserved for
masculinity. The pavilion is jealously guarded against
the unauthorized, yet everywhere there is thoughtful-
ness and convenience. There is no cheapness, no
makeshift arrangement at Lord's. All round the
ground rise adequate stands with fresh white paint
gleaming always upon seats and railings. Paths are
kept in faultless repair, lawns neatly cut and trimmed,
and flower-baskets brighten every dark corner. To sit
at Lord's is to share in substance and so become a
man of substance yourself.

The pavilion is surely the most magnificent of all
pavilions. Others may be larger, more lavishly
equipped—that I do not know—but Lord's stands
for me as the ideal. Graciously the stones have mel-
lowed with age, majestically the outline, flag-topped,
stands against the sky. Before is an enclosure, half-
way up there are balconies, and on the top is the very
perfection of grandstands.

Within, the Long Room, from which the play can
be watched through wide windows, is a storehouse of
cricketing treasure. Here exploration could take a

week, and would require the most enthusiastic and
knowledgeable of guides, for the exhibits are both
many and incredibly varied.

You may gaze upwards to oil paintings of past
legislators and players or old scenes of cricket, you
may note in the glass cases bats that bear but the
remotest resemblance to the modern implement,
stumps made from the wood of *H.M.S. Australia*,
ancient M.C.C. caps and ties, the original urn and
ashes of dispute, a solid ball of the notorious Bulli
soil, menu cards of historic occasions, and even torn
and broken coins that became entangled in the cutting machine.

Some of the relics will mean little to you, others
will strike sharp chords of memory, but no man calling himself cricketer could stroll the Lord's Long
Room without interest. Even the stairways that lead
to the balconies cannot be taken hurriedly, for the
walls are covered with photographs and notices, old
and new. Groups of teams that sailed the seas beneath M.C.C. colours in search of cricket fame;
Australians, South Africans, Indians who have
visited this country; score-cards of matches played
long ago yet remembered clearly, all are here to be
seen.

And on the balcony itself you may sit, surrounded
by tradition; you have only to keep quiet to be trans-
ported into yesterday. On your right the Eton and
Harrow match of goodness-knows-when comes under

review: 'Fine game, that, sir! Fine bowlers and
fielders those lads were. Reminds me, I saw So-and-
so the other day—Africa, I believe—no cricket now
—by gad, he's out. Beautiful catch, beautiful. I remember—" On your left. 'I don't know; these
modern cricketers seem to take things very easily.
Not the enthusiasm of our time, what! I've seen the
day when I've made a hundred—I think it was a
hundred, big score anyway—and then carried my
bag four miles to the station. Let's go and have some
lunch. Shall we?'

The needs of humanity apart from cricket are well
catered for at Lord's. Service and food are good and
adequate. Full luncheon or a sandwich and a drink
are equally easily obtainable. The appurtenances of
the game are in keeping with everything else. Score-
cards are always ready and up to date; the score-
boards go beyond bare adequacy, and everything is
done with dignity and efficiency. Even the wheel-
barrows are rubber-tyred.

Lord's is more than a cricket ground; it is an in-
stitution, a place where cricket is the very breath of
existence, and it stands as an example to all its
brethren of the game. That it should ever take second
place is inconceivable; its example may be followed,
should be followed, in many of the practical aspects,
but none other place on earth can have the atmosphere of Lord's.

As the years go by and new generations come to

tread its blessed turf they, too, will come under the spell ; they, too, will feel the irresistible ; they, too, will know beyond question that they have been within the royal palace of the kingdom of Cricket.

SOUTH AFRICA MAKE HISTORY

NEARLY thirty thousand people helped to make Lord's a wonderful sight on this Saturday of June. Lord's has always an atmosphere of cricket dignity, and to-day the sun shone from a sky of delicate blue and the breeze which ruffled the gleaming flannels of the players joined to make an unforgettable picture of this, the dearest of our games. All day long a pigeon fluttered or strolled in front of the pavilion, and when, at the fall of Dalton's wicket, the players were presented to His Majesty the King, the occasion touched perfection.

The South Africans began the morning in the best possible manner by winning the toss, and Mitchell found his highest form from the very first over, driving Nichols straight for three. Wyatt bowled from the pavilion end, and Mitchell had a boundary from an off-drive in that over and again an over or two later. Therefore, at 20, Hammond came on instead of Wyatt, and here Siedle was fortunate, for an experimental leg-break that failed gave him a four to leg. By noon the new ball was no more, and Mitchell bowled from the Nursery end, at once bringing a stir into the placid air. Siedle, by nature a most mistrustful batsman, was lured into believing a googly to be a leg-break, played a forcing back shot upon that assumption and was consequently bowled.

This must have been a serious blow to South African hopes, for Siedle is a big proportion of the solidity of the batting, and Mitchell and Rowan spent some time in quiet consideration of the state of affairs. Mitchell has a little habit of pulling at the left shoulder of his shirt with his right hand, which remark indicates that we are coming to regard him as amongst the great ones of cricket, for only to these do we do the honour of noticing their mannerisms.

Mitchell to-day fell away from his early mastery, chiefly because of some remarkably accurate bowling by Verity, whom neither batsman, easily and well as he played forward, could get away. An hour and a half passed by in the gathering of 59 runs, and then Nichols bowled again, and to immediate effect, turning one back sufficiently to beat the bat and have Mitchell leg-before. Nourse has been out of form in recent matches, and he never had time to become at home to-day. At ten minutes past one Verity had reward for much patient effort, Nourse not knowing whether to play back or forward, doing neither, and being bowled. This was indeed a poor morning for the South Africans, and they risked nothing further until lunch time, when their score stood at 79 for three.

Nichols and Verity began the afternoon's bowling,

but Verity could not find his earlier length, and Rowan, always a batsman looking for runs and never likely to refuse good gifts whether labelled 'full toss or 'long-hop', helped himself down the leg side and occasionally made precocious cuts off the stumps.

At 98 the fourth wicket fell, when Rowan, trying to turn Verity to leg, was given out caught at the wicket, Farrimond taking the ball very well indeed and thus ending an innings of which the roots seemed to have grown strongly and which was giving every sign of blossoming into a really fine flower.

The South Africans were in sore trouble now as Cameron came to join his captain, but with a man of Cameron's potentialities, and in such glorious form as at present, hope cannot but spring eternal. There was to be no disappointment, for with one boundary past point from Verity Cameron was off and away upon his joyous journey.

Nichols was brought back, presumably for the new batsman's especial benefit, but Nichols, Verity, Mitchell, and everyone else met with precisely the same reception. Cameron is a courteous batsman. There is no flourish in the swing of his bat, no flashing and leaping like the water of Lodore in his movements. When he hits you for six, he does so with the minimum of effort, as though to say 'I am afraid I must, but let us get it over quickly'. Nor does the wine of his own making go to his head. Cameron knows when to stop, and that characteristic probably puts him at the head of present-day hitters and accounts for his remarkably consistency.

To-day he had scarcely been at the wicket five minutes when Verity bowled him a full-toss and the ball finished amongst the leg-side spectators. Nichols was gloriously square-cut for four and Langridge (when he came on at the Nursery end) driven straight for four and pulled for six.

Cameron knows not the meaning of lost causes and knows bowling good only when it proves itself so. Of the 65 runs made in the first hour of the afternoon, Cameron had 40 for forty minutes' work. From 40 to 50 was a matter of two balls from Mitchell, one being driven into the pavilion and the other hooked from far outside the off-stump for four.

Wade was in the main a spectator and uncomplainingly so. But at quarter-past three he tried to drive Langridge and edged a catch to Hammond at slip. South Africa were 158 for five, and Dalton was the last recognized batsman to come. He began well with a good back shot and a mighty hook, each counting four, but so great was the spell, that we grudged him every moment for keeping Cameron inactive.

Actually Dalton made 19 good runs and looked likely to make considerably more until he hit a

full-toss straight back to Langridge and was well
caught. Here came the interval of presentation and
the end of South African hopes of a big total, for
though Cameron lived his partners were always
obviously fallible.

Balaskas escaped before he had scored, being
beaten by Langridge only for the ball to come
through too slowly for a stumping chance, but his life
was short, and he had but one boundary before
Verity bowled him.

Cameron put two hundred on the board with another grand off drive from Verity, and South Africa
had still four wickets in hand at tea-time, although
Mitchell had reason to feel aggrieved when Farrimond dropped the ball with Langton sprawling yards
from his allotted ground.

The tea interval, the new ball, some factor less
easily observed or a general combination served to
bring a quick ending to the innings. Cameron was
bowled in Nichol's first over—the applause alone
was an adequate commentary on his magnificent display—and three balls from Hammond were enough
for Langton and Bell. But for Cameron, of course,
the innings was a sad failure, an opportunity un-
seized, and a tragedy of inexperience against bowling
sometimes good, generally steady, but never devas-
tating.

England had eighty minutes' batting in the lovely
evening light, and made runs so easily that we are

justified in the expectation of a considerable first innings lead. The loss of Sutcliffe and Leyland gives
the South Africans reason for a pleasant Sunday
afternoon, but Wyatt has so far shown no disposition
towards dismissal, and Hammond has twice played
strokes descended straight from the form of his best
years.

Sutcliffe was out leg-before and to his evident surprise with the total at five, and Leyland went at
forty-six, bowled in the first over from Balaskas.
Wyatt had nearly all his runs on the leg side and
played the ball almost without fail in the middle of a
very straight bat.

To-day has been full of cricket of interest and
promise, but we must wait until Monday to know
with any certainty how the game is likely to finish.
Finish to the advantage of one side or the other it
certainly should.

SOUTH AFRICA
First Innings

B. Mitchell, lbw (n), b Nichols . . .	30
I. J. Siedle, b Mitchell	6
E. A. Rowan, c Farrimond, b Verity . .	40
A. D. Nourse, b Verity	3
H. F. Wade, c Hammond, b Langridge .	23
H. B. Cameron, b Nichols . . .	90
E. L. Dalton, c and b Langridge . . .	19
X. Balaskas, b Verity	4
A. B. Langton, c Holmes, b Hammond . .	4
R. J. Crisp, not out	4
A. J. Bell, b Hammond	0
B. 1, l.b. 1, w. 1, n.b. 2 . . .	5

Total 228

ENGLAND
First Innings

R. E. S. Wyatt, not out	37
Sutcliffe, lbw, (n), b Bell	3
Leyland, b Balaskas	18
Hammond, not out	12
L.b. 4, w. 1	5

Total (for 2 wkts) . . . 75

E. R. T. Holmes, Verity, Ames, Nichols, Mitchell (T.), Langridge (Jas.), and Farrimond to bat.

Fall of the Wickets

1	2
5	46

BOWLING ANALYSIS
SOUTH AFRICA

	o.	m.	r.	w.		o.	m.	r.	w.
Nichols	21	5	47	2	Mitchell	20	3	71	1
Wyatt	4	2	9	0	Verity	28	10	61	3
Hammond	5·3	3	8	2	Langridge	13	3	27	2

Mitchell bowled one wide and Nichols and Langridge each bowled one no-ball.

Fall of the Wickets

1	2	3	4	5	6	7	8	9	10
27	59	62	98	158	187	196	224	228	228

MONDAY

Another great crowd saw the South Africans play great cricket at Lord's to-day, and 6.30 found them 238 runs ahead with four wickets to fall. This would be no particularly strong position had we not seen England's fallibility against spin bowling—had we not seen batsmen struggling and tumbling this morning—but as it is there is a world of promise in to-morrow's cricket, and the South Africans at the moment hold the cards. If the weather plays a fair part, the match should certainly reach a definite result, and whichever way it goes the victory will be one of high merit.

England began the fair cricketing morning in the full knowledge that many first-innings runs were wanted to stave off the threat of a South African victory. Wyatt and Hammond were scoring at once, Hammond with a three to leg and Wyatt with a boundary in Crisp's first over, and Hammond had a lovely four past cover two overs later.

Balaskas bowled at the pavilion end from the day's beginning, and within a quarter of an hour Wade was relying entirely upon spin, for Dalton bowled instead of Crisp from the Nursery end. For twenty minutes the batsmen found everything as merry as a marriage feast, but no sooner was 100 on the board than Wade's faith in Dalton was given utter justification, for Hammond was bowled. The ball came off the pitch rather quickly and did not rise to the expected height, but Hammond's shot, half back, half cut, seemed careless.

Wyatt was never this morning in such ease as on Saturday, but after one or two faltering moments he made his 50 and then watched Ames suffer agonies of apprehension during an over from Balaskas in which Siedle seemed to waste a sharp chance at second slip.

At twenty minutes to twelve, Wyatt got himself out, hooking a long hop from Dalton with more force than discretion, for Nourse to come racing in from the square-leg boundary to hold a beautiful catch. Ames was always in evident distress, and in utter bewilderment at 116 he was thoroughly bowled by Balaskas, who was now not only bowling a length but turning the ball uphill with astonishing life.

After these England misfortunes there was more than a shade of relief in the clapping accorded to a good cover drive by Holmes off Dalton, but Balaskas was always a danger, and at 121 Holmes trod what was becoming a well-worn path back to the pavilion, Bell holding a good low catch at short leg.

Langridge and Farrimond had spurs to win, and for a while we had visions of this being their field of Crécy. They were uncertain and sometimes original in their shots, but gradually Langridge gained sufficient confidence to hit the ball in front of the wicket and Farrimond showed care and skill in choosing the ball to ignore.

By twenty-five minutes to one 150 runs were scored, but five minutes later Farrimond's plucky little effort came to an unlucky end, the ball going on to the stumps from pad and bat. Crécy faded from our minds.

Langridge went as far as 27 before reaching forward to Balaskas and giving the patiently waiting Mitchell his first opportunity of the innings. So, still 51 runs behind, England had only two wickets left, and at ten minutes past one the first of these went down as Nichols, injudiciously cutting, was neatly and surely caught at the wicket off Langton, who had been brought on instead of Dalton during the obstinacy of Langridge and Farrimond. Verity made runs with good shots and bad ones, but never in sufficient quantity to cause the South Africans much anxiety, and just before lunch the innings was all over for 198.

The morning was triumphantly South African. Balaskas bowled the whole two and a half hours with rare skill and enthusiasm, proved that his performance against Yorkshire was no mood of a golden Tuesday, and thoroughly deserved every wicket in his bag. Once again the England batting failed dismally against spin bowling that was allowed to pitch its own length, and away in Australia Grimmett and O'Reilly will chuckle reminiscently as they read the papers.

The wicket, of course, will receive most of the

blame, for we are inclined to believe these days that international batsmen cannot be expected to get runs on any wicket where the ball will swing or turn.

The afternoon's play, according to these lights, will need much explanation, for the South Africans not only built up a great lead but their batsmen played so well against all the bowling, plain or coloured, that England could produce, that there was never the least prospect of wickets tumbling. Both Mitchell and Siedle had boundaries in Nichol's first over, and as Hammond was treated with equally scant courtesy, 27 runs came in quarter of an hour before Mitchell (of Derbyshire) and Verity tried their hands.

There was a groan when a caught and bowled chance dropped from Mitchell's right hand, but the mistake was as inexpensive as it possibly could be, Siedle being caught at the wicket off the same bowler with no more runs scored. This wicket fell at quarter to three, and England had no other success until five minutes past five, by which time the South African total was 136.

Mitchell and Rowan looked long and earnestly at the bowling, found it wanting in the fundamental quality of good length, and stayed happily through the afternoon hours. Neither batsmen was unduly aggressive, yet there was no opportunity for sleep at any position in the field, and few overs passed without some good sound shot from Mitchell or some quick thrust of Rowan's impudent bat.

Once or twice Verity got the ball past Mitchell's
bat, but the covering pads were always in position,
and the bowlers received no more hope than they
could muster from an occasional tentative leg-before
appeal.   The Derbyshire Mitchell had a bad spell
from which the South African Mitchell helped himself to fours down the leg side, and 50 was up in
fifty minutes.   Mitchell's private 50 came at ten
minutes to four, and by this time runs were coming
so smoothly and well that the alarums and excursions
of the morning seemed a vague and unreal dream,
born of the summer heat.

There was a momentary stir when Verity sent up
the 100 with a ball that beat both Rowan and
Farrimond and which would have been a stumping
chance had it not gone down as byes, but at tea-time
South Africa were 117 for one, Mitchell 61 and
Rowan 37.

The blessed interval brought a change in the game,
for after two boundaries by Mitchell had made the
second-wicket partnership worth 100 Nichols had
Rowan lbw, and a grand little innings full of
confident cuts and strong drives was over. At last the
bowlers began to dictate, and South Africa passed
through a bad period in which four batsmen were
out and made only 5 runs between them.

Nourse failed again, and was bowled playing back
to Verity, Cameron hit high but not far enough, and
Ames at deep mid-off held the catch, Wade went

along precisely similar lines to Nourse, and Dalton was gently caught at silly mid-off.

Mitchell lived through these trying times with a calm and assurance which stamp him as great, and at twenty minutes to six a great roar of applause, deep and sincere, in recognition of a mighty achievement, marked the completion of his first Test match century in England.

This will surely remain Mitchell's day of days, for to score a first century at Lord's before thirty thousand people, with the game depending on the innings, must be every cricketer's dream. No subsequent 'ducks', no bad patches of seasons to come, could ever efface or dim this glorious memory. Let the day end on this note.

SOUTH AFRICA

1st Innings.		2nd Innings.	
B. Mitchell, lbw (n), b Nichols	30	not out . .	129
I. J. Siedle, b Mitchell (T. B.) .	6	c. Farrimond, b Mitchell (T. B.)	13
E. A. Rowan, c Farrimond, b Verity . . .	40	lbw (n), b Nichols .	44
A. D. Nourse, b Verity . .	3	b Verity . .	2
H. F. Wade, c Hammond, b Langridge . . .	23	b Verity . .	0
H. B. Cameron, b Nichols .	90	c Ames, b Mitchell .	3
E. L. Dalton, c & b Langridge	19	c Wyatt, b Verity .	0
X. Balaskas, b Verity . .	4		
A. B. C. Langton, c Holmes, b Hammond . . .	4	not out . . .	16
R. J. Crisp, not out . .	4		
A. J. Bell, b Hammond . . .	0		
Extras . . .	5		6
Total . .	228	(for 6 wkts.)	208

1	2	3	4	5	6	7	8	9	10	1	2	3	4	5	6
27	59	62	98	158	187	196	224	228	228	32	136	158	169	169	177

ENGLAND

1st *Innings*

R. E. S. Wyatt, c Nourse, b Dalton	53
Sutcliffe, lbw (n), b Bell . .	3
Leyland, b Balaskas . .	18
Hammond, b Dalton . .	27
Ames, b Balaskas . . .	5
E. R. T. Holmes, c Bell, b Balaskas	10
Langridge (Jas.), c Mitchell, b Balaskas	27
Farrimond, b Balaskas . .	13
Nichols, c Cameron, b Langton	10
Verity, lbw, b Langton . .	17
Mitchell (T. B.), not out .	5
Extras	10

Total . . 198

1	2	3	4	5	6	7	8	9	10
5	46	100	109	116	121	158	161	177	198

ENGLAND BOWLING

	o.	m.	r.	w.		o.	m.	r.	w.
Nichols .	21	5	47	2	Mitchell (T. B.)	20	3	71	1
R. E. S. Wyatt	4	2	9	0	Verity . .	28	10	61	3
Hammond .	5·3	3	8	2	Langridge .	13	3	27	2

SOUTH AFRICAN BOWLING

	o.	m.	r.	w.		o.	m.	r.	w.
Crisp . .	8	1	32	0	Balaskas . .	32	8	49	5
Bell . .	6	0	16	1	Dalton . .	13	1	33	2
Langton .	21·3	3	58	2					

Crisp bowled one wide.

TUESDAY

Beating England by 157 runs at Lord's to-day, the South Africans achieved a great triumph and fulfilled an ambition of many years' standing. Never before have they won a Test match in this country, and however the rubber may end or the tour progress 'Wade's team' is assured of a high place in history.

Their success in this second Test match was well earned from every point of view, and in every phase of the game the South Africans were England's superiors. Both the South African innings totalled more than did either of England's, a South African alone scored a century, and Cameron gave a glorious display of batting on the first day.

Langton and Balaskas always looked better bowlers than any of the men of England, and they made full use of a wicket which gave them assistance, but was never approaching the really impossible. In the field, too, the winners were more certain of their catching and more lively in their ground work. Finally, Cameron as a wicket-keeper had a polish quite absent in Farrimond's work.

This is no time for regrets. We have been fairly and squarely beaten. That is not a matter for abject sorrow so much as an indication that we are not making the most of our own talents. One match does not make a rubber, and if we appreciate the real strength of our opponents there is still time to remedy the omissions of the past. To-day we drink to South Africa. To-morrow we set our own house in order.

The South African innings this morning was mainly a matter of consolidation, a buttressing of walls already built, and the work rested entirely upon two men, for so soon as a wicket fell the innings was declared closed at 278 for seven wickets.

It is no particularly creditable reflection upon the bowlers of England to realize that it took them an hour and thirty-five minutes to dispose of a batsman marked No. 9 on the card, and although there were occasions when Langton was smiling bewilderment and a catch or two went to ground, it was always quite easy to picture the stand assuming the proportions it did.

Mitchell was this morning in his fine form of yesterday, and after a long and careful examination of the pitch decided that batting could be both possible and pleasant. He was in no hurry, and Nichols and Hammond with the new ball received merited respect, but run was added to run with a stately assurance that will make Mitchell's name ever memorable at Lord's.

Hammond did not bowl at all badly; several times he beat the bat with balls that lifted quickly, and an edged shot from Langton found Holmes at fault in the slips, but England got no nearer than that to the wanted wicket.

Verity, Langridge, and Mitchell all bowled within a short space of time, but with them neither batsman was in any sort of trouble, Mitchell having a boundary from a beautiful square cut off the Derbyshire Mitchell, and Langton off-driving Verity for four.

Steadily and confidently the scoring went on, little bursts of clapping from the South African enclosure marking the achievement of this and that minor record until at twelve thirty-five Langton pulled

Hammond to the leg boundary, and the seventh wicket partnership was worth a hundred. Then everyone clapped. The very next ball brought Hammond some return for his labours, the bowler himself taking a low catch with his left hand.

Mitchell, not out, with the second highest score ever made by a South African in a Test match, had the sweetest of serenades all the way home, and passed from a scene which left the score-board showing his side 308 runs to the good and the clock allowing nearly four hours and a half for play.

From the England point of view, the morning served merely to confirm an impression that had crept upon us yesterday when we felt the bowling scarcely adequate to its task. Our attack must have more concentrated venom, as opposed to Micawber-like fatalism, in the Test matches to come.

Wyatt and Sutcliffe (and a runner) saw the quiet, safe passage of the forty minutes before lunch, and then began the final thrilling stages in the sunshine of the afternoon. Balaskas bowled at once, but this time from the Nursery end and thus again into the wind, which had changed completely round since yesterday morning, and at 24 he had the first wicket, Wyatt playing a very short ball on to his foot, whence it rolled to the off stump. This perhaps was sheer good fortune for the South Africans, but the gods were not to be entirely with them.

At thirty-two Sutcliffe edged Bell to short fine leg,

where Rowan would have had the easiest of catches had he not slipped and so made his work at once difficult and a failure. For an hour and a quarter after this accident Rowan's skies must have seemed one unbroken stretch of grey.

Leyland, of whom much was expected and still more hoped, achieved practically nothing, for Crisp, on in place of Bell at the pavilion end, beat and bowled him in his first over and England were forty-five for two at ten minutes to three.

With Hammond in, Sutcliffe became almost entirely and almost impregnably defensive, but Hammond saw the ball well from the first and made good shots off his back foot and to leg. He had two beautiful boundaries in succession off Langton, one past third man and the other to fine leg, and in forty-five minutes forty-four runs were put on. This was but a gesture, a flicker of the flame before the fire became damped, but we did not know it at the time, and we found Hammond's moments golden, and Sutcliffe's bat a welcome prop and stay in time of trouble.

Langton had been put on at the pavilion end when the score was 77, and at 89 he bowled his leg-break to a perfect length, and Hammond, playing forward, just touched it for Cameron to appeal triumphantly and successfully.

If the South Africans had ever lost heart (a state of affairs in no way evident at any time) the fall of this mighty one brought them vigorously back to life.

From this point until tea-time they were no longer strugglers but conquerors in their own right, and Langton showed us magnificent bowling.

At quarter to four the sun broke through Rowan's particular clouds, for Sutcliffe played back to a ball that kept low and was lbw. There shall be no suggestion that Sutcliffe's injury was responsible for his dismissal, but there can be no question that his innings was played under a severe handicap, and we must recognize with gratitude that he stayed for two hours and ten minutes and accord him much praise even allowing for the missed catch.

English applause welcomed the hundred up at ten minutes to four, but five minutes later with two runs added Holmes was bowled by a fast yorker, and very shortly after Ames was lbw to a ball that turned back so sharply as to be quite literally unplayable.

Langridge and Farrimond found sympathy in each other's distress for some twenty minutes, but once again Wade made a happy bowling change, and Crisp removed Farrimond's off stump with a lovely ball. So at tea time England had seven wickets down, and the interval proved an artful assistant, for Langridge was lbw to the second ball of the evening.

The South African victory was clearly written now and the end no more than a matter of time. Verity found a long hop from Balaskas and put it away to the leg boundary, but 8 runs was his limit, and Balaskas had him caught at second slip at 149.

A few minutes after five o'clock it was all over, and the crowd swarmed upon smiling tourists and surged to the front of the pavilion to cheer the South African captain to the echo as he appeared on the balcony saying 'Thank you'.

SOUTH AFRICA

First Innings		Second Innings	
B. Mitchell, lbw (n), b Nichols .	30	not out . . 164	
I. J. Siedle, b Mitchell . .	6	c Farrimond, b	
		Mitchell	13
E.A.Rowan, c Farrimond, bVerity	40	lbw (n), b Nichols .	44
A. D. Nourse, b Verity . .	3	b Verity . .	2
H. F. Wade, c Hammond, b			
Langridge	23	b Verity . .	0
H. B. Cameron, b Nichols .	90	c Ames, b Mitchell .	3
E. L. Dalton, c and b Langridge	19	c Wyatt, b Verity .	0
X. Balaskas, b Verity . .	4		
A. B. Langton, c Holmes, b			
Hammond	4	c and b Hammond .	44
R. J. Crisp, not out . . .	4		
A. J. Bell, b Hammond . .	0		
B. 1, l.b. 1, w. 1, n.b. 2 .	5	B. 3, l.b. 5 .	8
Total . . .	228	Total (for 7 wkts dec.) . .	278

ENGLAND

First Innings		Second Innings	
R. E. S.Wyatt, c Nourse, b Dalton	53	b Balaskas . .	16
Sutcliffe, lbw (n), b Bell . .	3	lbw, b Langton .	38
Leyland, b Balaskas . .	18	b Crisp . .	4
Hammond, b Dalton . .	27	c Cameron, b Langton	27
Ames, b Balaskas . . .	5	lbw (n), b Langton .	8
E. R.T. Holmes, c Bell, b Balaskas	10	b Langton . .	8
Langridge (Jas.), c Mitchell, b			
Balaskas	27	lbw (n), b Balaskas .	17
Farrimond, b Balaskas . .	13	b Crisp . . .	13
Nichols, c Cameron, b Langton .	10	not out . .	7
Verity, lbw, b Langton . .	17	c Langton, b Balaskas	8
Mitchell (T.), not out . .	5	stCameron,bBalaskas	1
B. 4, l.b. 5, w. 1 . .	10	L.b. . .	4
Total	198	Total . .	151

BOWLING ANALYSIS
SOUTH AFRICA
First Innings

	o.	m.	r.	w.		o.	m.	r.	w.
Nichols .	21	5	47	2	Mitchell .	20	3	71	1
Wyatt .	4	2	9	0	Verity . .	28	10	61	3
Hammond .	5·3	3	8	2	Langridge .	13	3	27	2

Mitchell bowled one wide and Nichols and Langridge each bowled one no-ball.

Fall of the Wickets

1	2	3	4	5	6	7	8	9	10
27	59	62	98	158	187	196	224	228	228

Second Innings

	o.	m.	r.	w.		o.	m.	r.	w.
Nichols .	18	4	64	1	Langridge .	10	4	19	0
Hammond .	14·4	4	26	1	Holmes .	4	2	10	0
Mitchell .	33	5	93	2	Wyatt .	4	2	2	0
Verity .	38	16	56	3					

Fall of the Wickets

1	2	3	4	5	6	7
32	136	158	169	169	177	278

ENGLAND
First Innings

	o.	m.	r.	w.		o.	m.	r.	w.
Crisp . .	8	1	0		Balaskas .	32	8	49	5
Bell . .	6	0	16	1	Dalton . .	13	1	33	2
Langton .	21·3	3	58	2					

Crisp bowled one wide.

Fall of the Wickets.

1	2	3	4	5	6	7	8	9	10
5	46	100	109	116	121	158	161	177	198

Second Innings

	o.	m.	r.	w.		o.	m.	r.	w.
Crisp . .	15	4	30	2	Mitchell .	2	0	11	0
Bell . .	12	3	21	0	Langton .	11	3	31	4
Balaskas .	27	8	54	4					

Fall of the Wickets

1	2	3	4	5	6	7	8	9	10
24	45	89	90	102	111	129	141	149	151

Umpires : E. J. Smith and Walden.

THE DAYS OF THE WEEK

ONE who is perhaps the greatest of our modern essayists has touched charmingly upon the character of the days in the town week, and he being himself a cricketer I feel sure that I have his forgiveness for this adaptation of his theme.

The days of the cricketing week are very clearly defined in their character, and generally speaking we know what to expect if we note the date on the sporting page as we approach the ground. There is, of course, such a delightful element of uncertainty about the game itself that occasionally things do not plan out according to the calendar, but there can be no accounting for this by mortal rules and regulations. Sometimes we get Friday cricket on a Tuesday or even, on rare occasions, on a Thursday.

Saturday is the most important day of the cricketing week. All the battles of the county giants start on Saturday, and the larger crowds seem to bring out the very best from the players. In addition a good performance is all the more desirable on Saturday, because there is the whole of Sunday for glorious retrospect, and never bloom the roses in the garden more sweetly or never the shade of the trees more graciously cool than in the atmosphere of yesterday's hundred. Saturday, of course, is the democratic day ror cricket. Not all of us can spend mid-week hours in the sunshine, but on Saturday we can all watch and idolize and wonder without a care in the world beyond our own entertainment and the success of our particular heroes.

Monday is a business-like day. It is very often a long day's play, because hours have to be adjusted to travelling arrangements, and Monday invariably comes in for the overtime. On this day we expect much sound, persevering cricket with the inevitable end of the match in sight, when stumps are eventually drawn. We expect strong, insistent play with one side forcing its will upon the other. There is no froth and foam on Monday's cricket; it is all good, solid eating.

Tuesday is the dullest day of the week ; Monday's match simply ends on Tuesday, and the day is chiefly useful in providing a few hours for passing from one ground to another. Without delving into a mass of statistics, which can be made to prove or disprove anything, of how many dramatic finishes can you think which took place on a Tuesday? Of course not —the very nature of the day is all against such incidents.

Wednesday is definitely a good day. It is Saturday in miniature, lacking only the finishing touches which make Saturday so peerless. The best matches may not begin on Wednesday, but there is always something thrilling in the start of any match, and when giant meets pygmy, incident is rarely lacking, and sometimes that incident is not without sensation. Some take their weekly half-holiday on Wednesday, so that, too, is an asset to the character of the day.

Thursday is of unstable character. You never know what to expect of it. Sometimes it can be as solid as Monday, but more often it is an affair of kaleido-scopic change with peculiar single events having a big effect upon the final pattern. On Thursday it is possible to snatch an off hour at the cricket and leave well satisfied that the day has not been entirely in vain. I would never trust a Thursday; it is the prophet's bugbear and the critic's trap, and even the greatest of cricketers or cricket teams are liable to behave unexpectedly under the influence of Thursday's inconstancy. Women's cricket, in theory at any rate, should always be played on Thursday.

Friday is the day for excitement. There is the week end in prospect, another period of toil has almost passed by, and cricketers are all eager and agog. Perhaps that is why there are so many good finishes on Fridays. Contrary to the belief in civilian life, Friday is not unlucky for cricketers, and there are as many happy memories of Fridays as of any other day in the week. It mingles something of the joys of achievement and anticipation, and the pity of it is that so few of us have the opportunity of enjoying Friday to the full.

There is a certain attractive fickleness about Friday

which, however exasperating at the time, draws us inevitably back with the most sanguine of hopes. However long and hard the drought, there is always a chance that Friday will break it, and time and again we have been led up the garden path to the most intriguing of finishes and then left in the cold while the rain fell from tantalizing skies.

And here we are with our mackintoshes and our luncheon packets, passing through the gates again on Saturday morning.

BUSINESS AND PLEASURE

IN days far distant when a rough-carved branch, the stump of a tree, and a simple sphere were the implements of the game, cricket was purely recreative and no other factor than pure enjoyment entered into its objects.

To-day cricket has developed far beyond the imagination of its early players and has become an affair of intense importance to half the civilized world. The fortunes of a few flannelled men upon a green field are responsible for the state of mind of thousands of people in different quarters of the earth. The game has become a business, a means of livelihood to hundreds, and the principal item of news in the daily journals of the British Empire. No longer is bat and ball the pastime of the idle hour, unpremeditated and immediately forgotten.

There is a very real danger that the essence of simple enjoyment will be driven from our cricket, whether played upon international arena or in the field of Farmer Johnson. There is more than a suspicion that our games and their results are becoming invested with too much seriousness and that in a complicated age enjoyment is becoming dependent upon sensationalism.

How many cricketers, players, and spectators, of

to-day are satisfied with quiet hours beneath the sun, happy in the careless freedom of contented minds, unwearied because this wicket or that does not fall or this batsman or that does not achieve a century?

How many of our players are not slaves to the occasion carrying always upon them the weight of a wearying responsibility and seeking ever 'the bubble reputation'? How many men go day by day from the pavilion rejoicing only in the feel of bat or ball in the hand, without ever a thought of the morning's publication of the averages, 'the world forgetting by the world forgot' in the purely intrinsic pleasures of cricket?

It is, I should imagine, impossible ever to retrieve the lost simplicity of games; money, personal success, partisanship, and future prospects are now too inevitably bound up with cricket to be disentangled and set aside. Cricket need be no worse for their intrusion, always provided that these factors never become predominant.

There is still great joy to be had from the playing of cricket of all grades, but before that joy can be fully experienced the simplicity of pleasure must be wholly appreciated. From the joy of the player comes the joy of the spectators and there would be no complaint of dull and worthless cricket were every player to radiate his own enthusiasm for participation.

Too many of our cricketers bring solemnity and gloom in their very walk down the pavilion steps.

Too often does a batsman feel aggrieved if it be suggested to him that a boundary is a happy creation and a century not so much a matter of duty as an expression of well-being.

Too many bowlers display obvious misery upon being asked to bowl for more than half an hour at a time, and to the last ounce of effort. Too many fieldsmen regard the non-batting hours as a necessary penance to be undergone with the minimum of exertion.

We do not ask genius from all our cricketers; we do not (or we should not) demand historic deeds upon every summer's day. We would rather have an hour's honest enjoyment than a week's pained effort. We want our batsmen to be thankfully conscious of their own ability and ever ready to display their talents for their own and our delight. We want our bowlers to use all their energies in bowling for bowling's own sake, independent of scoreboard readings or the day of the week. We want fieldsmen to seek and to know always 'the finishing touch of an honest brown hand.'

A truly first-class cricketer is not one who condescends to appear before us and perform because he is expected to do so. The greatest technician is an empty shell and a bore beyond compare without the willing spirit, and the most desperate 'rabbit' radiates pleasure and inspiration if his endeavour be earnest and whole-hearted. The cricketer himself finds his greatest happiness in simplicity of aim; there are those who cannot go upon the field without worrying hour upon hour over the tactics of the captain and suggesting this move or that as more suitable to the requirements of the situation. There are those who cannot sit as spectators for half an hour without dwelling upon the incompetence of the present as compared with the past, and airing views and knowledge to a totally uninterested neighbourhood.

The happiest cricketer is he who, on the field and off, accepts without complaint the gifts of the moment, neither dwelling lingeringly upon yesterday nor dreaming idly of to-morrow. No day passes upon a cricket field without some joy is brought to someone and no day passes without some pleasure lost for want of seeking.

The greatest cricketer, to himself and his companions, does his immediate task to the best of his ability and with cheerful willingness; obvious endeavour is the most lovable characteristic of any player of any game, and more of it in modern cricket would go far towards the solution of all the problems that beset us.

Whether cricket be well or badly played, let it at least be always enjoyed, for we know in our heart of hearts that the 'trier' is

> " The happy warrior . . . he
> That every man in arms would wish to be."

TWO AUSTRALIANS, 1934

D. G. Bradman and W. H. Ponsford, batsmen of Australia, have at least one characteristic in common; they amass huge scores. Fifty to them is merely indicative of the playing-in period safely passed, the century but 'a milestone along the road to progress, the end of the journey lying every beyond'. Time and again these batsmen have made scores of over 200, not infrequently they have passed the 300 mark, and innings of 400 and more are not unknown to them.

Batsmen cannot make such big scores with such consistency without having something in common in their method, and in the case of Bradman and Ponsford the common factor is their determination. Determination to succeed in their self-appointed task makes them forego the delights of ordinary batsmen, makes them ignore or quell the craving for one wild glorious moment leading inevitably to destruction, and keeps them along the same road all the time.

For them there is no wandering in the fragrant bypaths of big sixes and improbably unorthodox shots. They have their limitations, of which they are fully aware, and they never venture beyond the boundary fence of their own proved ability to dabble in the prohibited lands of uncertainty. Thus, and thus only, are great scores made with regularity.

But with this much in common, Bradman and Ponsford then diverge widely in matters of detail. Test match spectators have had rare opportunity to study the difference between these two men, for this year they have been together in two stands which developed into affairs in which the only records left to be broken were their own.

Bradman is unquestionably the greater batsman of the two. Ponsford is always a little hesitant in starting; there is always a certain straining of his eyes and tentative pushing of the bat at the start of his innings, and there is always a period when the bowler can delude himself into believing that he might easily get Ponsford out.

With Bradman there is no such hesitation. If he is to play a big innings, the signs are there from the first; without any delay or preamble he is hitting the ball in the middle of the bat and scoring runs with contemptuous ease. Nobody who saw those two back shots in the first over on that memorable Saturday at Leeds could help but read the writing on the wall or fail to appreciate its significance.

Bradman deals safely and profitably with balls that Ponsford makes no attempt to master. It is very doubtful if there is any batsman in the world who hits so hard as does Bradman the ball, of whatever pace, pitched only just short of a length on or outside the leg stick. Not for Bradman the swift covering up movement and the bat loosely held lest the ball spring off into the waiting leg trap. He stays where he is in line with the ball and, timing his shot to the last fraction of a second, hooks with all the incredible power in his wrists. Were he to miss the ball he would himself be hit, but that accident occurs very rarely indeed.

For this particular ball, Ponsford has no counter. He could, no doubt, play the usual defensive back shot and risk a simple catch to short leg, but he invariably prefers to turn his back and allow the ball to hit him in a manner which has more than once drawn derisive and scornful laughter from the spectators.

Ponsford apparently admits his inability to deal with this particular ball, and rather than risk losing his wicket in attempting to master it, he prefers to suffer what must amount to considerable physical pain. In view of these methods one can readily appreciate that leg-theory as bowled by Larwood, and as bowled by anyone else, is a distinctly variable quantity.

Not that Ponsford is without many good shots; he cuts delightfully and as safely as anyone can cut, but he has this stroke under control and reserves it for the appropriate ball; never will he cut at anything not simply asking to be cut.

Bradman does not cut as late as does Ponsford. He requires less time to see the ball and prefers to play it more towards (and invariably past) point, the ball leaving the bat with the speed of a bullet from a gun. Generally speaking, all Bradman's shots are played harder than Ponsford's, because Bradman's timing is so immeasurably superior.

Ponsford gives the impression of playing forward more than Bradman; Ponsford plays forward as a defensive measure without any intention of making a scoring shot. To such balls Bradman finds an extra instant in which to play a forcing shot off his right foot, the ball generally going towards mid-on.

Bradman goes forward to drive, and drives with a full swing of the bat, hitting the ball with tremendous force through the covers, but rarely straight. Ponsford is more sparing in his use of the drive, waiting patiently for the half-volley, without ever going to look for one on his own.

Bradman, of course, is far and away the more beautiful bat. Where Ponsford crouches at the wicket, Bradman stands upright, creating no impression of tenseness and strain, simply as a monarch surveying his all. Ponsford can become boring to watch, but Bradman, because of the miraculous power and perfection of timing, holds the interest to the end.

It may seem that Ponsford does not come out too well from the comparison. Let it be remembered that it is only a comparison, and however superior in technique and attraction Bradman may be, Ponsford must have proved to his own and the satisfaction of everyone else that he knows a thing or two concerning the scoring of runs.

AUSTRALIA'S ASHES

From quarter past eleven this morning, which was approximately the time at which Woodfull won the toss, until the drawing of stumps at half-past six, it was Australia's day at the Oval.

Through the intervening hours England toiled beneath a hot sun with but two widely separated consolation prizes to show for all their labour and endeavour; and there must have been moments of pure unadulterated misery when all hope of eventual success had departed, and the struggle seemed an impossible one of dwarfs against Titans.

Yet to the everlasting credit of English cricket, let it be said that these men never flagged, that they found the strength and will power to fight to the end, and that one of them achieved a 'bumper' at twenty minutes past six.

But for all England's bravery the triumph went to two men of Australia, who came together at twelve o'clock and stayed through the sunshine of the day to make the biggest partnership ever Test cricket has seen.

We thought Bradman and Ponsford incredibly marvellous at Leeds, but—goodness, gracious!—they were only having some practice for this. As far as I know every record went by the board, and these two green-capped delights even went so far as to break more records than most of us knew to be in existence.

But it was not in their records that their magic chiefly lay. They were not so wonderful in what they actually did as in the certainty and absolute mastery of the methods they used.

From the very beginning they set themselves to put Australia in an unassailable position, and all personal endeavour was devoted to that end alone. Fifty meant nothing, centuries meant nothing. It was the the total that was of supreme importance, and, with that consideration in mind, no unnecessary risk was taken, and there was no suspicion of playing with fire.

Winning the toss meant a great deal on this paradise of a wicket, and to Australia it must have seemed that 'all the world was fair and young again' when Ponsford and Brown opened the innings to Bowes and Allen.

There was no early incident, no sensational roar of astonishment, and by noon the game had just settled comfortably down when Clark came on at the Vauxhall end for Bowes to change over. In that first over of his Clark slipped in a magnificent ball which seemed to turn back just a shade. It was too good for Brown, and beat his defensive bat to hit the top of the off and middle stumps and remove a most dangerous batsman.

Most of us were so delighted at this early success that we scarcely noticed a slim, hunched-up figure come to the wicket, take guard, and proceed with the game. The first time we were really aware of Bradman was when he edged Bowes past second slip for the first four of the match. Perhaps Bradman was aware of this sense of neglect and, if so, much of his subsequent behaviour should teach us in no uncertain manner that hosts must look more closely to the arrival of their guests.

Just at this point Ponsford was not altogether confident in himself, and although he had a four to fine leg off Clark that bowler worried him more than a little.

Bradman soon made himself at home and comfortable by hitting Bowes very well past cover to the boundary, and in the same over he had another four from a fierce intended hook which, in some strange manner, found itself passing between mid-on and the bowler. Bowes handed over to Hammond, from whom Bradman took a perfectly timed four to leg, and, lo! and behold, fifty runs were on the board before we knew where we were.

Clark had had an exceptionally good spell, but gave way at fifty-eight to Allen, to whom Ponsford gave short shrift, having a magnificent four past point and two successive boundaries through the slips, the second, in particular, being a really fine shot.

Hammond contrived to bowl a maiden to Bradman

before Ponsford came to his fifty at five minutes to one, and when Verity bowled Bradman took no unnecessary risk, but got a forcing shot away to the leg boundary.

Noon saw a wicket fall, and one p.m. might have seen another; for Ponsford turned Allen hard to leg, where Wyatt, although getting his hands to the ball, let it go as he spun round. 'Hard luck,' we thought, but how hard we had no manner of guessing. Verity bowled a second not unexpected maiden to Bradman, but another lovely four through the covers from the batsman participant in this little duel saw the 100 up at five minutes past one, and at lunch there were 123 runs on the board—Ponsford 66. and Bradman 43.

Bowes bowled from the pavilion end after lunch. Bradman restarted the scoring with his famous forcing back shot (a boundary, of course), and at 2.20 reached 50 with a most glorious shot past cover off Clark.

Ponsford gave England a faint gleam of hope when he edged Bowes through the slips, Woolley just touching the ball with his outstretched right hand, and he was clearly unhappy with anything in the nature of a 'bumper'. Bradman, however, made a remarkable shot off one such ball, falling away from the wicket and hitting a boundary with the bottom of the bat far higher than the handle at the moment of contact.

Twice in one over no-balls from Clark counted four to Ponsford. Bradman was particularly severe on that bowler, cutting and driving him with astonishing and contemptuous ease.

Somewhere around three o'clock Hammond and Verity were in charge of the attack. This was the first time that all the fast bowlers had been out of action together, and possibly as a mark of appreciation, Bradman made a perfect late cut off Hammond to send up 200. It was a perfect shot, all done so neatly and quickly and easily as to be a thing of pure undiluted joy.

And now the attention swung over to Ponsford, who had unostentatiously crept into the nineties, and at a quarter past three we saw him complete his century with a single off Bowes. Then came the new ball, which, after having been disparagingly hooked to the boundary by Bradman, became a devilish instrument in the hands of Clark.

He bowled an inspired over to Ponsford, beating the batsman three times without being lucky enough to touch the edge of the bat, and, with Bradman in some momentary difficulty with Allen, there appeared more likelihood of a wicket falling than at any other period of the day.

Bradman passed the landmark of his century at twenty-five minutes to four. Gradually the threat of the new ball passed away, and, with patriotic hearts well-nigh sick with hopelessness, yet our cricketing souls filled with delighted appreciation, we watched the batsmen come once more into superb domination and score with ever-increasing ease and freedom.

Not until 256 did the batsmen make another mistake, and then Ponsford was lured into Verity's trap and played the ball to mid-off, where Wyatt dropped a catch he would certainly expect, and be expected, to hold in the ordinary way; and, as if to rub salt into the wound, Ponsford touched a rising ball in Allen's next over and gave Woolley, at second slip, a chance he might well have taken, but didn't.

All this must have been dreadfully disheartening for the bowlers who, fortunately deprived of a glimpse of the future, though doubtless their imaginations were not idle, toiled gamely on with both energy and skill.

The half-hour between four and four-thirty saw Bowes and Verity steady the scoring, saw 300 up, and saw Bradman, who had long since overtaken Ponsford, make his individual total 150 just on the interval.

After tea the unceasing procession of runs moved on, ever more stately, ever more speedy; bowlers reached the stage when they altered the field more from sheer desperation than anything else, and over by over the Australians built up a total that ceased to be a cricket score and became a mathematical monument.

The runs piled up so solidly and inevitably that even Bradman's mishits, rare as snowstorms in June, were scoring shots. Wyatt bowled, Leyland bowled, almost everyone bowled. For some time we marked the passing of landmarks and records with punctilious applause, but eventually that pastime palled, and we could raise but the mildest of cheers when Bradman hit Verity for six.

And then, when most of us 'bitterly thought of the morrow', Bradman was out. He made a shot at a bumper from Bowes—a bumper at twenty minutes past six, and the score 472 for one wicket—and as the ball sailed high above his head, he touched it on to Ames. As he walked to the pavilion with one 6 and thirty-two 4's to his name, I thought of all the glorious batting I have ever seen, and none in its certainty and power came near to threatening to overtop this. I have exhausted my vocabulary on Bradman. He is Bradman, and that must suffice.

Ponsford remains to continue on Monday. Him, were it not for his records, I could possibly forget, for his genius is not that of Bradman; there are in him human frailties, in his armour chinks that will widen with the passing of time, but that he is a great batsman there is no shadow of doubt.

And what of the men of England? This was never their day, and we can only hope and pray that their sufferings will have given them the strength and the courage to fight on to the end; that the vision of victory in prospects so gloomy will be all the more gloriously pure and shining; that, undaunted and skilful, they will achieve such as mortal man has never before.

To-day the bowling was not so unworthy as the score would suggest, and Clark was the best of them all. He had pace, he had fire and direction and, all things considered, his luck was by no means of the best. The others were good without being great, and each gave signs that, with things going their way, they were not out of their class.

The dropping of catches was unfortunate, tragic if you will, and, as it happened, alarmingly expensive, and the ground fielding decidedly other than perfect; but there has been drought at the Oval, and the outfield is unusually rough, and that explains several little lapses.

As at Leeds, Wyatt has held back the third new ball and, as at Leeds, it may not be without effect when it is used on Monday. Let those who stayed away, and there were many, for the crowd was surprisingly small and inhumanly quiet, not despair for England yet. The match has a long course to run.

AUSTRALIA
First Innings

W. A. Brown, b Clark . . .	10
W. H. Ponsford, not out . . .	205
D. G. Bradman, c Ames, b Bowes . .	244
S. J. McCabe, not out	1
B. 1, l.b. 8, w. 2, n.b. 4 . .	15
Total (for 2 wkts) . . .	475

Fall of the Wickets

1	2
21	472

MONDAY

As the sixth ball of the final over passed at the Oval to-day a great sign of relief went round the ground, for England had made an excellent beginning in their reply to Australia's big score.

Walters and Sutcliffe remain unconquered, and start to-morrow with the knowledge that almost 100 runs have been chipped from their opponents' total, and with a pleasantly comfortable feeling that all the bowlers who matter have been seen and comfortably dealt with.

On the whole the honours of the day are even, and, despite the appearance of the scoreboard, there was much to give satisfaction to the most fervent of England supporters. Again much of the luck ran Australia's way, and again England's bowlers toiled bravely for in adequate reward.

Some of the Australian batsmen had all the luck they could possibly have hoped for, yet, despite this, none was good enough to make a really monumental sculpture on the foundation stone so well and truly laid by Bradman and Ponsford on Saturday. Some-one else should surely have made a century but, truth to tell, no one looked like doing so, and there were very few minutes when the fall of a wicket seemed beyond the possibilities of hope.

Before play began there was sufficient light rain to necessitate the production of the covers, but, beyond the customary few minutes for no reason at

all, play was not delayed, and Allen began from the
Vauxhall end, taking the new ball and his first over,
and giving McCabe the opportunity to put it past
Wyatt to the fine leg boundary.

Clark bowled to a leg trap from the Pavilion end,
indeed, he could scarcely help doing so, whatever
may have been his inclinations, for a strong breeze
blew directly across the ground and made leg-theory
a virtuous necessity from one end.

By the second over Allen had worked up his best
pace, and the fourth ball so completely beat McCabe
that the middle stump went whirling from the
ground in a splendid cascade. Judging by the shot,
or rather lack of it, McCabe never so much as saw
that particular delivery.

The cheers for Allen's feat had scarcely died away
by the time Woodfull appeared on the scene. For
him Allen strengthened the slips to four, but he took
away a man for Ponsford, which was unfortunate,
because Ponsford had a boundary off the edge that
would have provided an easy catch for anyone in
position. Indeed, he edged two in succession, the
second taking the total to 500, but then Allen earned
more applause for two maidens. Allen bowled this
morning like a man with energy and to spare, even
though no-balls extended the length of every other
over.

Clark, too, bowled with life and fire, but the batsmen achieved uncomfortable survival, and Hammond

and Bowes had to take over the attack. Quite literally it was the bowlers who attacked, for there was no trace of the batsmen's domination of Saturday, and it was not until Ponsford took three fours in one over from Hammond that there came an interruption in the quiet spell.

Bowes had Woodfull guessing and 'feeling for them' all the time, and as for Ponsford, he would have none of him, and to anything showing signs of rising he fluttered, possibly disdainfully, certainly very hurriedly, away. But Bowes just lacked the skill or luck, call it what you will, to put on the finishing touch to his work. Gradually the tension relaxed as the batsmen's vision grew clearer and their state of mind more contented, and another lucky escape for Ponsford sank any hopes of a wicket.

When his score was exactly that of Bradman, Ponsford made a sort of semi-cut at Bowes and gave Verity in the gully a right-handed catch which Verity dropped. Immediately afterwards Woodfull had a four off Verity which started as a square drive and finished somewhere behind Ames.

One o'clock saw Ponsford reach 250 with a lovely square cut, and five minutes later Clark came on for Bowes who, some of us thought, might well have been rested before this. Clark bowled to six men, from Bowes at point to Hammond at first slip, and he bowled very fast; but the only effect was to bring the scoring to a standstill, and it was not until

1.20 when Allen went on, that there was further
incident.

Ponsford had a boundary off Allen's first ball, a
boundary that Verity could possibly have stopped,
but that same over saw his end. He drew away from
a rising ball and either hit or trod on his own wicket,
much to his obvious disgust. If ever a man got himself out, Ponsford did on this occasion, and in view
of his methods the dismissal was no more than poetic
justice poetically just.

Two hundred and sixty-six is a great score, no
matter how many chances may have been given, and
in making the most of such luck as came his way
Ponsford gave himself everlasting memories of
what is reputed to be his last Test Match
innings in England. For Australia he fought,
and his triumph is hers, and we accord him due
honour.

Kippax joined Woodfull after lunch and straight-
way placed Clark past mid-on to the boundary with
as neat a shot as one could wish to see, but Woodfull
was amazingly lucky. Without giving an actual
chance, he flicked at off balls and could not touch
them, and time and again he tried to turn Clark to
leg for the ball to slide safely away through the slips.
He it was who put up 600 when an overthrow to the
boundary added 5 to his score.

Kippax lived dangerously but with delicately
traced beauty; all the time he was making full shots

at the ball where the others were restraining themselves in case of something unexpected at the last
minute. When he is at the wicket he is batting all
the time, and if such life involves brevity it is unquestionably brave.

Woodfull had one more slice of luck before he was
out. He edged Bowes high over the slips to the boundary and was bowled by the next ball. It may perhaps be unfortunate to fall at 49, but Woodfull can
scarcely complain on this particular occasion.

Bowes had a good spell hereabouts, for shortly
after three o'clock he had Kippax leg-before, and at
a quarter past he knocked back Chipperfield's middle
stump, this last being no surprise at all, for Chipperfield was distinctly unhappy throughout his short
stay.

Oldfield and Grimmett took considerably more
moving than we expected (or was it rather hope than
expectation?). Oldfield made a really fine hook to
the boundary off Bowes, and later achieved an en-
trancingly delicate late-cut. Allen had to be recalled
to bring about a separation, but his wretched luck
continued when Grimmett edged him to Verity at
third slip, and Verity let fall a catch which came
to him breast high. However, Allen did get the
wicket in the end, Grimmett touching the ball on
to Ames at five minutes past four.

The end was in sight, the cool restfulness of the
pavilion almost an accomplished fact, though it took

some time before Allen could induce a ball to hit Ebeling's stumps. They missed the leg stump, missed the off and went over the top with such depressing regularity that at last Allen thought, 'Well, they can't very well go underneath,' and hit the foot of the leg stump.

O'Reilly stayed long enough to allow Oldfield to prove what a valuable number eight he can be by driving Verity straight and turning Allen for boundaries, and O'Reilly himself had an all-run four to make the total 700 before Clark at long last finished off this innings of disaster for England.

The bowling analyses are things to haunt the poor men in the rough nights of winter, but then the memory of their brave toil and their ill-luck in the matter of the appallingly bad work of their assistants should serve as some measure of solace. How many catches went to ground I do not propose to count, but if this match is lost there will be no need to look further for the reason.

England's innings began at five minutes to five, and Walters started it in encouraging fashion with a four to leg in Ebeling's first over. Both he and Sutcliffe began with astonishing confidence. How they stood there unconcernedly and played easily what seemed to our distorted imagination the most deadly bowling in the world defies the understanding of us poor mortals, huddled up beneath the grim shadow of a score of 701.

Walters played beautiful cricket. He had another lovely four past mid-off, from Ebeling, and then turned back to McCabe and put him away to the leg boundary with a touch of exquisite timing. Within twenty-five minutes of the start Walters was 30 and Sutcliffe 3, a state of affairs worrying no one less than Sutcliffe, for whom the years seemed to roll away back to 1924–5 in Australia, when he had but to pick up his bat to be sure of a score.

At twenty minutes past five Grimmett came on for McCabe, and one more over from Ebeling saw that bowler give way to O'Reilly of the contortionist action and sinister mien.

O'Reilly at once bowled a no-ball to give Sutcliffe his first 4, and a bad ball down the leg side gave the batsman another boundary—so safely hit as to typify the Test Match Sutcliffe to perfection.

Forty minutes' play saw 50 on the board, but at 51 there was a moment of breath-taking terror and a genuine shriek of agony from some distressed soul when Walters, in trying to force Grimmett to leg, put the ball only just short of mid-on. A three to leg off O'Reilly completed Walters' 50, and how we hoped and prayed that he would go on in his own sweet way, neither hastened by success nor made desperate by the magnitude of the task as yet scarcely begun.

Sutcliffe was a heart-breaking paradox. He made these Australian bowlers look horribly menacing, and then played them calmly and gently with unshakable belief in himself and his powers. All manner of traps were set for him. Men were brought to silly mid-off and mid-on, Grimmett tossed the ball high and then kept it low, but Sutcliffe took his singles in his own good time and occasionally restrained Walters' inclination towards impetuous running.

'No,' said Sutcliffe decisively on more than one occasion, and probably added to himself, 'Why the hurry? We shall be here to-morrow and the next day, and well—I hope to see this thing through to the end.'

Sutcliffe played O'Reilly out of action and brought Ebeling back at ten minutes past six, and then dealt neatly and profitably with the fast bowler by putting him to leg for 2, 4, and 3.

In the last forty minutes of the day Walters saw very little of the bowling, and whether this was by accident or design it worked out very well for England. O'Reilly had one last attack, one last great effort to entrap one of these men who mean so much to England's chances; but breathless as were the minutes of anxiety, and cruel as the delayed agony between each delivery, the end came at 90 for none as the shadows grew long on the grass and the sparrows came twittering on to the outfield to claim the Oval for their own evening games.

AUSTRALIA

W. A. Brown, b Clark	.	.	.	.	10
W. H. Ponsford, hit wkt, b Allen		.	.	.	266
D. G. Bradman, c Ames, b Bowes		.	.	.	244
S. J. McCabe, b Allen	.	.	.	.	10
W. M. Woodfull, b Bowes	.	.	.	.	49
A. F. Kippax, lbw, b Bowes		.	.	.	28
A. G. Chipperfield, b Bowes		.	.	.	3
W. A. Oldfield, not out	.	.	.	.	42
F. V. Grimmett, c Ames, b Allen		.	.	.	7
H. I. Ebeling, b Allen	.	.	.	.	2
W. J. O'Reilly, b Clark	.	.	.	.	7
Extras	.	.	.	.	33
Total	.	.	.	.	701

ENGLAND BOWLING

	o.	m.	r.	w.
Bowes .	38	2	164	4
Allen .	34	5	170	4
Clark .	37.2	4	110	2
Hammond .	12	0	53	0
Verity .	43	7	123	0
Wyatt .	4	0	28	0
Leyland .	3	0	20	0

Fall of Wickets

1	2	3	4	5	6	7	8	9	10
21	472	488	574	626	631	638	676	682	701

ENGLAND

C. F. Walters, not out	.	.	.	.	59
Sutcliffe, not out	.	.	.	.	31
Total (for no wkt.)		.	.	.	90

TUESDAY

The third day's play is over, and Australia lead England by 566 runs and have still eight of their second innings wickets to fall. If that plain statement is not an accurate pointer to the result of the match the greatest cricketing miracle in history must happen at the Oval.

Fighting all the way against misfortune almost as powerful as their opponents, it is to be hoped that England will go on fighting, game to the last, and crushing from the bitter leaves of defeat some faint redeeming fragrance which will linger through the chill days until her sun shines again.

England's ill-luck persisted to-day to such an extent that two of her men were incapacitated, one of them in the course of successful accomplishment, but there was more than luck to account for the morning collapse, and the plain truth of it is, luck or no luck, England's batsmen failed in spirit and technique before a deadly attack made more venomous by success.

The serious business of the day began promptly at 11.30 when Grimmett bowled from the Pavilion end to Sutcliffe. O'Reilly continued at the Vauxhall end and, in his first over, Chester called a no-ball so quickly that Sutcliffe had ample time to make a perfect cover drive to the boundary. Singles took the total to 99, and the first-wicket partnership became worth 100 at twenty minutes to twelve, when Grimmett beat Walters and Oldfield (a sufficiently rare occurrence to be noteworthy in itself), and the ball went for four byes.

There were actually no signs of strong and confident batsmanship from Walters this morning, but it was Sutcliffe who was the first to go, he being most beautifully caught close up on the leg side off

Grimmett. Probably no other wicket-keeper in the world would have taken such a catch, and for that reason Sutcliffe may count himself unfortunate: but that must be poor consolation.

Woolley had a wonderful, unnerving reception on his approach to the wicket, and he got away with a single from his first ball, but at ten minutes to twelve the second wicket fell when Walters was out. He made a wretched shot, hitting at O'Reilly without getting anywhere near the pitch of the ball and so gave mid-on an easy catch which Kippax accepted with due gratitude. Thus were gone both heroes of last night and but a paltry 18 runs added.

Woolley himself fell with scarcely a murmur of protest, playing O'Reilly very tamely to McCabe at short leg. He turned from the wicket as 'an old man broken with the storms of state', and carried back to the pavilion all our hopes of lovely Kentish runs flowing from a bat in complete domination of an attack which has all too long got wickets from the dressing room window.

These three wickets fell in one of the blackest half-hours England cricket can ever have known, and there was more than a touch of relief in the applause for Wyatt's first scoring stroke—a boundary hook from O'Reilly—followed two balls later by an even more powerful shot of similar type and to the same effect. Hammond had a glorious off-drive through the covers from O'Reilly, but several overs passed

anxiously by before there came another opportunity
for a boundary hit, and then Wyatt swept a full toss
from Grimmett to leg.

Time passed but slowly. There was embryonic
menace in everything done by the Australians, and
the greatest crowd of the three days sat in a silence
pregnant with nervousness. This, we felt, was
England's vital hour, and at half-past twelve Wyatt
played on to Grimmett. There was scarcely a hand-
clap as the bails fell, and the Australians assembled
round Grimmett in a congratulatory ring. The whole
ground was intensely quiet with exquisite pain, borne
as bravely as could be. True, there was no need
for us to suffer, no need for us to watch, but, fasci-
nated by fatality, we scarcely dared to take away
our eyes from the middle for an instant.

Hammond gave us a chance to relieve our pent-up
feelings when he turned Grimmett prettily to the leg
boundary, and at twenty minutes to one O'Reilly's
magnificent spell came to an end. In case we were
foolhardy enough to congratulate ourselves on the
removal of one danger we were quickly reminded of
another, for in his first over Ebeling had Hammond
caught at the wicket, the batsman playing an unnecessary back shot to a ball it seemed he might
reasonably have ignored. Hammond has had such
a bad time in this series of Test Matches that all the
time this morning we deluded ourselves that he was
bound to make a big score, and for this reason alone

his dismissal was cruelly cutting, inhumanly hard to bear.

And so we turned to Leyland as the saviour of our fading hopes, and wished and wished (as though that would do any good!) that a white rose might bloom strongly through the tempest of destruction all around us.

Leyland was in for more than a quarter of an hour before he scored, but then he played forward to Ebeling like a strong man and true, and mid-off ran a losing race to the boundary with the ball. In fact, this began quite a burst of scoring from Ebeling and encouraged Ames to jump in to Chipperfield and hit him mightily through the covers.

So far everyone but Leyland had been fighting for their runs, and taking them only in a spirit of apology, but Leyland scored much more at his own inclination and with definite assertion of his absolute right to do so. In this way, and with Ames dealing easily with Chipperfield, the horrible nightmare of recent events began to melt into the distance and become shadowy and unreal until we looked at the scoreboard and came to the sharp realization that England were not yet 200 and five wickets were down.

Grimmett, of course, had to come back to look into this situation, but Ames played the ball and not the bowler's name, and a late cut for four put up 200 just after twenty minutes past one. Leyland, too, sweetened the lunch hour by hitting O'Reilly high into the empty outfield for 4 and 3, and was 40 at the interval, his partner 28.

Grimmett and O'Reilly bowled after lunch and Ames very soon made a grand back shot off Grimmett, the ball passing between cover and extra-cover as a red line searing the brown turf. Leyland, before lunch, had observed the pathetically empty outfield and did something to remove the desolation by another 4 to leg off O'Reilly, and after a hard and profitable hook he completed his 50 with an impudently short single.

For the first time to-day we could shift about in our seats seeking a comfortable pose to watch what we had sought for so long.

'Alas, the vanity of human wishes!' The imps of mischief who pursued us all the day found a further thorn for our discomfort. With the total at 227 and his own score 33, Ames suddenly bent double in obvious pain and, after a moment's solicitous attention from Leyland and the Australians, he limped from the field, his bat, once so bravely fluttering a banner, now trailing despondently beside him. Subsequent inquiry revealed him to be suffering from an acute attack of lumbago. Lumbago at this point, with England striving in her death throes! Was ever fortune more unkind to a cricketer than this?

Even Leyland felt the bitterness of fate for a moment and seemed to lose something of his superb confidence. But his heart is too big and his love of the fight too great for him to give way to despair, and in a flash he was himself again when he hit O'Reilly far over the leg boundary for six.

Allen wasted no time in contemplative pre-liminaries. Whenever he could he played straight down the wicket like a man with infinite faith in the fundamental straight-forwardness of human nature, and he cracked a full toss from Grimmett to the boundary as one saying, 'Yes, I know what to do with that.'

When Ebeling came back instead of O'Reilly Allen put his first ball past cover for 4, so Ebeling called for the new ball, and Allen placed it for a single to put up 250 (at the hour of two-fifty) and Leyland square cut it to the boundary.

McCabe's first over to-day was just about as bad as it could be, and almost every ball of the six counted runs including one particularly fine slash past point by Allen. But that batsman's brief, bright effort came to an end at three o'clock, when Ebeling just removed the off-bail with what was possibly an in-swinger. Curiously enough, Allen had been very nearly bowled twice previously by just such deliveries, and he himself having expressed amazement at his continued existence it was rather surprising to find him making no better effort, no effort at all, in fact, to play the fatal ball.

When McCabe had bowled his regulation over or two Grimmett took over from him, and was immediately driven straight and hard to the pavilion rails by Leyland. By this time, I need scarcely say, there was no fanciful arrangement of 'silly' fieldsmen; mid-on and mid-off were half-way to the boundary when Leyland was batting, and there they saved a run or so, but even then only when Leyland failed to get the ball in the middle of the bat. There is much to be said for the old adage 'A man bowls only as well as he is permitted', and Leyland, more than any modern England batsman I know, invariably gives the saying practical illustration.

Ebeling's very useful spell ended at 276, O'Reilly relieving him, and it was off this bowler that Verity made his first move with a big hit to the leg boundary. Verity scored only in spasms with long but perfectly satisfactory intervals of quietude, but Leyland went steadily on, although Grimmett found a rough spot off the wicket, and turned one ball so sharply as to hit Leyland on the elbow.

Leyland got into the nineties with another leg hit to the boundary off O'Reilly, and from the next ball Bradman had a desperate and always hopeless chase for a skier in the long field. In the same over a sweet leg-glide for 4 put 300 on the board and took Leyland to 98.

A lovely shot past cover off Grimmett at last brought him to one of the greatest centuries Test cricket has ever seen, and I write the phrase with the full consciousness of its implication and the danger in the modern tendency (*sic*) to exaggeration. The skill and the power of his shots, his amazingly comforting confidence, and the dreadful pit from which this flower of an innings blossomed, make the effort one worthy of the highest possible praise. Maurice Leyland is unquestionably England's greatest Test Match batsman at the present time.

Scarcely had the cheers for his century died away than the gallant Verity played on to Ebeling, who had just taken the place of O'Reilly. Verity had stayed, looking thoroughly at home, for fifty minutes, and was rather unlucky to be out as he was; he had held up an end as one brother Yorkshireman for another, and in view of the slender batting resources to come, his innings was worth more than the mere runs it counted in itself.

Verity knew better than we did how slender was the batting to follow, for it was only when Clark came to the crease that we learnt that Bowes was ill and unable to bat, and, with Ames quite incapable of resuming, the end was very near at hand. Actually Leyland got himself out hitting at Grimmett, and England were 380 runs behind.

The score sheet tells that the Australian bowlers were too good for the England batsmen, and so they were, but there was more than a suspicion in many of the strokes that the batsmen in question

were fully aware of the fact before ever they came
to take guard. Perhaps this is being ungenerous
to the bowlers, but we can say with perfect certainty
that the Australian fielding was far and away better
than England's, Brown and Bradman being the
biggest stars in a constellation that shone very
brightly.

It was a strange-looking England eleven that took
the field at twenty minutes past four. Woolley was
keeping wicket, and Gregory and McMurray (of
the Surrey Club) were fielding. Allen and Clark
starting the bowling, and in Allen's second over
England started her bad first innings work again
when Walters, at deep point, dropped the easiest
of catches offered by Ponsford. This was too much
for Allen, so he himself gave a demonstration to his
failing colleagues when Brown popped up a ball
into Clark's leg-trap and Allen darted forward to
hold a low catch with his right hand.

Bradman came in to give Ponsford another little
demonstration, this time in how to deal with short
balls of uncertain direction. Where Ponsford turned
his back amid the jeers and boos of a long-suffering
crowd, Bradman flashed a hook at the very first
ball and the leg trap ducked to safety as the ball
flashed by to the boundary.

Half an hour's intensive campaign of considerable
inaccuracy left Ponsford very unhappy indeed, and
after several miraculous survivals against Allen, he

played Clark into the leg-trap, where Hammond brought off a handsome catch low down.

And that was the extent of England's success, though Sutcliffe refused a difficult chance offered to the slips by McCabe from an Allen whose stout heart must have been well-nigh breaking.

Both Bradman and McCabe settled down to a mood of quiet mastery, the chief spark of delight for England being the fielding of McMurray, who drew wave upon wave of applause for his brilliant work in the field.

The batsmen took every advantage of anything loose—and there was much—and after Bradman had come without the slightest mishap to his 50, the end of the day was sheer agony for England, with McCabe completing his 50 at 6.25 to put the seal on Australia's superiority.

AUSTRALIA

	First Innings		*Second Innings*	
W. A. Brown, b Clark	.	. 10	c Allen, b Clark .	1
W. H. Ponsford, hit wkt, b Allen		266	c Hammond, b Clark	22
D. G. Bradman, c Ames, b Bowes	. . .	. 244	not out .	. 76
S. J. McCabe, b Allen	.	. 10	not out .	. 60
W. M. Woodfull, b Bowes	.	49		
A. F. Kippax, lbw, b Bowes	.	28		
A. G. Chipperfield, b Bowes	.	3		
W. A. Oldfield, not out	.	. 42		
C. V. Grimmett, c Ames, b Allen		7		
H. I. Ebeling, b Allen	.	. 2		
W. J. O'Reilly, b Clark	.	. 7		
B. 4, lb. 14, w. 2, n.b. 13	33		B. 20, l.b. 5, w. 1, n.b. 1 .	. 27

Total 701	Total (for 2 wkts) 186

ENGLAND
First Innings

C. F. Walters, c Kippax, b O'Reilly . .	64
Sutcliffe, c Oldfield, b Grimmett . . .	38
Woolley, c McCabe, b O'Reilly . . .	4
Hammond, c Oldfield, b Ebeling . . .	15
R. E. S. Wyatt, b Grimmett . . .	17
Leyland, b Grimmett	110
Ames, retired hurt	33
G. O. Allen, b Ebeling	19
Verity, b Ebeling	11
Clark, not out	2
Bowes, absent ill.	0
B. 4, l.b. 3, n.b. 1	8
Total	321

BOWLING ANALYSIS
AUSTRALIA

	o.	m.	r.	w.		o.	m.	r.	w.
Bowes.	38	2	164	4	Verity .	43	7	123	0
Allen	34	5	170	4	Wyatt	4	0	28	0
Clark .	37·2	4	110	2	Leyland .	3	0	20	0
Hammond .	12	0	53	0					

Clark bowled two wides and six no-balls ; Allen six no-balls, and Bowes, one no-ball.

Fall of the Wickets
First Innings

1	2	3	4	5	6	7	8	9	10
21	472	488	574	626	631	638	676	682	701

Second Innings

1	2
13	42

BOWLING ANALYSIS
ENGLAND

	o.	m.	r.	w.		o.	m.	r.	w.
Ebeling	21	4	74	3	O'Reilly .	37	10	93	2
McCabe .	6	1	21	0	Chipperfield .	4	0	22	0
Grimmett .	49·3	13	103	3					

Ebeling bowled one no-ball.

Fall of the Wickets

1	2	3	4	5	6	7	8
104	108	111	136	142	263	311	321

WEDNESDAY

Australia beat England by 562 runs at the Oval to-day and so won the 'Ashes'. They won because they were vastly the superior of two teams, neither of which could by any stretch of imagination be called great.

Australia's claim to fame lay in the possession of a batsman named Bradman, who was ably assisted in his work by another named Ponsford, two bowlers, Grimmett and O'Reilly, who are good bowlers made great by England batsmen, and the best wicket-keeper in the world. England were a fine team on paper—that is paper printed before the beginning of the match—but in this game several reputations received a nasty jolt like unto toppling some from their thrones.

To put it optimistically, there was little hope for England this morning, and, although the remaining Australian wickets, thanks to some fine and plucky bowling and fielding, went down comparatively cheaply, again the England batting was woefully weak, and almost from the beginning of the final innings the end was in sight.

Bowes provided an heroic touch when he declared his intention of playing and bowling, and he soon gave proof that even the bowling of an unfit Bowes is something to be remembered. After Verity had bowled the opening over from the Vauxhall end, Bowes at once took off his sweater, and, with his second ball, clean bowled Bradman, knocking the leg stump from the ground with a ball that came much more quickly from the pitch and kept lower than Bradman's hook shot could anticipate. His first spell was only brief, and Allen came on to take the new ball at 204, Clark bowling instead of Verity.

From Clark, McCabe had a fine hook to the boundary, but the next ball he played hard to cover, where Walters held a brilliant catch, taking at his feet a ball which was moving so quickly that most of us never realized a wicket had fallen until McCabe walked away.

More quick bowling changes followed, when Bowes came back for Clark at a quarter past twelve and Clark relieved Allen fifteen minutes later. Both changes were immediately successful, for with his second ball Bowes yorked Woodfull, and off Clark Kippax pulled a ball high to long-leg, where Walters confidently and quietly took a good catch.

Kippax had made some delightful shots without getting the full reward for them, but he did find one gap in the covers when he made an off-drive from Bowes.

Another five minutes saw the next wicket fall, for Oldfield never even started to settle down before he edged Bowes to Hammond at second slip. And England were taking catches this morning.

Chipperfield and Grimmett made a tantalizing little stand for the seventh wicket, Chipperfield

achieving more than one handsome shot before
Woolley took a most professional catch at the
wicket at five minutes to one. Grimmett lived
dangerously all the while. Twice he slashed at
rising balls from Bowes to see the shots sail high
over the slips, but the third time paid for all, and
Hammond held a head-high catch in his best
manner.

There were distinct possibilities of the end of the
innings before lunch, but Ebeling and O'Reilly
contrived not only to stay, but to achieve some
measure of comfort. Ebeling at least succeeded in
doing what no one else had done to-day when he
drove Bowes straight for four, and not even bowling
changes had the desired effect.

Even after lunch neither batsman showed much
inclination to get out, and in all 45 runs were put on,
no mean consideration were it not that the exact
total had long since ceased to matter greatly. At
half-past two Bowes gave himself an equal share of
the wickets with Clark when Allen took a simple
catch at square-leg, and England were left wanting
708 runs to win.

Bowes was magnificent. To bowl at all was no
inconsiderable feat, but to bowl sufficiently well to
take five good Australian wickets, two of them
clean bowled, for a comparatively insignificant
55 runs, was a feat worthy of comparison with the
great deeds of other days. Bowes may not be the

best fast bowler in England, but he is undoubtedly
one without whom no England team should take
the field, and we must wish him a speedy and complete recovery from his illness that he may continue
to delight us.

Seven hundred and eight was an immense score to
face, and I do not think that anyone had even the
vaguest hope that England would come anywhere
near that total. Certainly we hoped and expected
that a sterling and prolonged fight would be put
up, but the story of the end makes sorry reading for
the enthusiast's eyes. The disasters began almost
at once, for within ten minutes of the start McCabe
got a faster ball past Walters and bowled him.
McCabe, if you please, who is only supposed to
bowl at all for the purpose of wearing the shine from
the ball! In his next over he had another wicket
when Woolley made a half-hearted hit and gave
Ponsford at deep mid-off an easy catch. This was a
tragic ending to the Test career of one of England's
most beautiful and successful cricketers, and it was
a sad and forlorn figure that passed from the field
to the accompaniment of a few sympathetic hand-
claps.

McCabe, of course, had now done his work (more
than his work, some of us were inclined to think), and
when Grimmett bowled in his stead Hammond had
the first four of the innings with an off-drive past
Bradman.

Ebeling's long spell ended at half-past three, when O'Reilly took his place, though only 17 runs had come in these forty-five minutes, and his advent saw more rapid movement on the scoreboard.

Sutcliffe had a four from a none-too-well-timed pull from Grimmett, but when he repeated the shot a few balls later there was in that much more certainty and power. Hammond caused silly mid-off some consternation when he ran out and hit O'Reilly hard to the on-boundary, and not all the vehemence of O'Reilly's appeal for lbw. off the next ball got him any satisfaction from Chester.

It was about this time that England made her one and only showing towards fight. Sutcliffe had two good fours in one over from Grimmett, a pretty cut and a sweep to leg. Hammond had an off-boundary from O'Reilly and an all-run four from a shot past point, and then gathered himself in all his majesty and brought off a glorious on-drive to the pavilion enclosure.

At 56 Hammond, then 29, should certainly have been out one way or another. He ran down the pitch to hit Grimmett, but misjudged the ball, which went past him to touch Oldfield's gloves and be fielded by first slip. It seemed from my particular view-point that Hammond just touched the ball, which may possibly account for Oldfield's failure to gather it, and to our vast relief and surprise Hammond scrambled back. In our relief there was the bitterness of irony. 'Why, oh why,' we muttered savagely, 'did this sort of luck not come our way before the clouds of hopeless despair gathered so thickly around, while there was still competitive interest in this match?'

At ten minutes past four Ebeling bowled for O'Reilly, Grimmett, of course, persisting at the Vauxhall end, and after Sutcliffe had echoed his swan song with another sweep to the leg boundary he did what he had been threatening to do for some time, the ball sliding gently off the edge of his bat to McCabe close at hand in the gully. Sutcliffe was gone, three wickets were down, and Grimmett came very near to smiling.

Leyland came in to thankful applause for services rendered, and, having watched Hammond drive Ebeling straight for four, himself took two successive boundaries to leg from the unconcerned Grimmett. A vicious short ball from Ebeling was equally viciously slashed past point by Hammond, and that brought the breathing space of a tea interval in which to speculate as to whether or not the match would last out the day.

Hammond gave the unbelievers reason for congratulation on their judgment in O'Reilly's first over after the resumption, playing the ball rather nonchalantly back for the bowler to make an equally nonchalant, but irrevocably final, left-handed catch.

If the end were not obvious before, it was written plain for all to see now.

Wyatt put up the 100 by running out and driving Grimmett over mid-off's head. Leyland hit with all his might at anything he could reach, and when he was out at ten minutes past five he went in a fine frenzy of cricket. He hit the ball hard and low to cover. Brown stretched out his hands as the ball was going away from him, let it go, and recovered it to bring off a really great catch. Leyland smiled as he saw the ball finally held, and in that smile there was everything that is fine in cricket.

At 5.25 Wyatt passed from the scene, caught by Ponsford at mid-on in trying to pull Grimmett, and the end hastened on. Verity went in precisely the way as had Sutcliffe, Bowes had one hit for a desperately run two, and then put O'Reilly straight to Bradman at square-leg, and a fine flurry and cloud of dust indicated the stumping of Allen at five minutes to six. Allen made some good shots, two of them especially fine on-drives in succession from O'Reilly, and as he ran from the field, he threw a captured stump to an Australian, whom he thought would treasure it more dearly than he himself could do.

Very quietly the crowd assembled in front of the pavilion, very modestly the cheers rang out for the conquerors, and very dolefully most of us passed from the Oval.

AUSTRALIA

First Innings		Second Innings	
W. A. Brown, b Clark	10	c Allen, b Clark	1
W. H. Ponsford, hit wkt, b Allen	266	c Hammond, b Clark	22
D. G. Bradman, c Ames, b Bowes	244	b Bowes	77
S. J. McCabe, b Allen	10	c Walters, b Clark	70
W. M. Woodfull, b Bowes	49	b Bowes	13
A. F. Kippax, lbw, b Bowes	28	c Walters, b Clark	8
A. G. Chipperfield, b Bowes	3	c Woolley, b Clark	16
W. A. Oldfield, not out	42	c Hammond, b Bowes	0
C. V. Grimmett, c Ames, b Allen	7	c Hammond, b Bowes	14
H. I. Ebeling, b Allen	2	c Allen, b Bowes	41
W. J. O'Reilly, b Clark	7	not out	15
B. 4, l.b. 14, w. 2, n.b. 13	33	B. 37, l.b. 8, w. 1, n.b. 4	50
Total	701	Total	327

ENGLAND

First Innings		Second Innings	
C.F.Walters, c Kippax, b O'Reilly	64	b McCabe	1
Sutcliffe, c Oldfield, b Grimmett	38	c McCabe, b Grimmett	28
Woolley, c McCabe, b O'Reilly	4	c Ponsford, b McCabe	0
Hammond, c Oldfield, b Ebeling	15	c and b O'Reilly	43
R. E. S. Wyatt, b Grimmett	17	c Ponsford, b Grimmett	22
Leyland, b Grimmett	110	c Brown, b Grimmett	17
Ames, retired hurt	33	absent, ill	0
G. O. Allen, b Ebeling	19	st Oldfield, b Grimmett	26
Verity, b Ebeling	11	c McCabe, b Grimmett	1
Clark, not out	2	not out	2
Bowes, absent, ill	0	c Bradman, b O'Reilly	2
B. 4, l.b. 3, n.b. 1	8	L.b. 1, n.b. 2	3
Total	321	Total	145

BOWLING ANALYSIS
AUSTRALIA
First Innings

	o.	m.	r.	w.		o.	m.	r.	w.
Bowes	38	2	164	4	Verity	43	7	123	0
Allen	34	5	170	4	Wyatt	4	0	28	0
Clark	37·2	4	110	2	Leyland	3	0	20	0
Hammond	12	0	53	0					

Clark bowled two wides and six no-balls, Allen six no-balls, and Bowes one no-ball.

Fall of the Wickets

1	2	3	4	5	6	7	8	9	10
21	472	488	574	626	631	638	676	682	701

Second Innings

	o.	m.	r.	w.			o.	m.	r.	w.
Allen	16	2	63	0	Verity	.	14	3	43	0
Clark	20	1	98	5	Bowes	.	11·3	3	55	5
Hammond .	7	1	18	0						

Allen bowled one wide and two no-balls, Bowes and Clark one no-ball each.

Fall of the Wickets

1	2	3	4	5	6	7	8	9	10
13	42	192	213	224	236	236	256	272	327

ENGLAND
First Innings

	o.	m.	r.	w.			o.	m.	r.	w.
Ebeling	21	4	74	3	O'Reilly	.	37	10	93	2
McCabe	6	1	21	0	Chipperfield		4	0	22	0
Grimmett .	49·3	13	103	3						

Ebeling bowled one no-ball.

Fall of the Wickets

1	2	3	4	5	6	7	8
104	108	111	136	142	263	311	321

Second Innings

	o.	m.	r.	w			o.	m.	r.	w.
Ebeling	10	5	15	0	Grimmett	.	26·3	10	64	5
McCabe	5	3	5	2	O'Reilly	.	22	9	58	2

O'Reilly bowled two no-balls.

Fall of the Wickets

1	2	3	4	5	6	7	8	9
1	3	67	89	109	122	138	141	145

HAMPSHIRE

OF all the pleasant journeys Michael and I have made in search of cricket I think I shall remember longest that which took us out of London upon the Great West Road and sent us into Hampshire on our way to Bournemouth. In the City the heat and dust and petrol fumes were almost unbearable, and there was mental relief, too, in our departure, for national pride had suffered in the spectacle of over-whelming defeat in a Test Match.

We were glad to see the end of London, glad to pass from the roaring confusion of the traffic to quieter ways and simpler scenes. Each passing mile brought the relief of peacefulness, and in the heat of the August afternoon we ran into that forest which was rightfully called New 850 years ago. The New Forest has history within its straggling bounds; there William the Second of England met strange end, but this day we did not seek the Rufus Stone that marks the scene of his fall. This day we followed in content the road that winds between great avenues of trees, turns corners to come upon open commons or fantastic-looking inns. Memorials and show places meant nothing to us when we had the sunlight streaming through the trees to lay designs upon the grass, when here and there the picnic-parties spread themselves luxuriously in sun or shade, when every now and then fleet ponies started upon our approach and fled from before us.

To the best of my recollection the journey was without event; nothing we did, nothing was done to us. Yet all my days I shall remember the New Forest that August afternoon and shall count the memory among the most precious of my store.

Bournemouth was our journey's end on that occasion, and Bournemouth then we saw at its best, for the sun shone and blue skies formed a background for the colours of the town. Bournemouth's character is in the air; its lovely beach, its pines, its woody hinterland are but appurtenances and secondary to the Bournemouth air. When you breathe Bournemouth you breathe lazy holidays, hours of idleness upon the sands, leisurely strolls and quiet days upon the sea. To hurry over anything in Bournemouth is a crime, a crime comparable to smoking with the port. You *can* be energetic in Bournemouth, and I daresay you can be energetic with pleasure and profit, but then, you *can* smoke with your port. As the spas of the world heal physical troubles by soothing away pain, so Bournemouth, spa of the mind, heals mental weariness by soothing away worries and anxieties. It is almost worth while being ill to be sent to Bournemouth for recuperation. What delight, then, to know

Bournemouth without the inconveniences of convalescence.

Bournemouth is Hampshire's playground; there are cities in the county more concerned with the business of the world, yet who would suggest less fascination in work than in play—when the work is the privilege of someone else? Southampton and Portsmouth have their business on the seas; theirs is a life of great ships, of comings and goings from and to the ends of the earth. Southampton, the important, the busy, rushing, noisy Southampton of to-day, is of recent growth, and came to its wealth when speed became the predominant factor of the age. It is the nearest great port to London, and there the wonder ships of the mercantile marine rest awhile to disgorge and take on their human cargoes. The great ships of Southampton are unforgettable: sleek and enormous, they rise from the dockside, worlds within a world, before they hurry away across the ocean along paths as well defined as a railway line.

If you go 'Below Bar' you will come upon these 'monsters', 'leviathans', 'ocean greyhounds'—all the metaphors are jaded now—lying quiescent yet dominant over all the city. They are Southampton's wonder; and to see the impatient little tugs set them off upon their way is the greatest gift the city can offer you.

Portsmouth always gives me the impression of

being slightly contemptuous of Southampton; there is an aristocratic raising of the eyebrows about Portsmouth whenever Southampton's name is in mention. 'Yes, yes, presumably Southampton uses the sea; we own it,' seems to come distinctly from every quayside and every lamp-post in historic narrow streets. There is, perhaps, some reason in the attitude, for the ships of Southampton sail because of the might of the ships of Portsmouth. Portsmouth has been in England's story since England's ships sailed the seas. Everywhere in Portsmouth Naval history urges itself compellingly upon you.

In Portsmouth George Villiers, Duke of Buckingham was stabbed to death as he prepared to set out upon an expedition for the benefit of his monarch, Charles I. In Portsmouth lies preserved and open for your inspection the best-known ship in all the world, Nelson's *Victory*. The *Victory* is out of the water now, but all her history remains within her. You are shown the cramped and stuffy cabin where England's Admiral lived, the very table he used, polished to shine like sunbeams, stands before you, and you marvel as you are told that in time of battle the furniture was thrown overboard and towed behind to make more room for business.

You are shown the corner where the dying Nelson lay, you are shown the guns his sailors fired, and you are taken up on deck to the sacred spot of the British Navy. It you inspect the *Victory* among a crowd you will be impressed; if you are fortunate enough to inspect it at leisure and be given time for thought you will feel, be it ever so faintly, the call of the sea; you will be conscious and proudly conscious of the heritage that is yours.

Everything in Portsmouth has the atmosphere of the Navy and its traditions. If you go to the cricket ground you will see there an amazing contraption officially designated the 'heavy roller'. It was built by Naval engineers; only Naval engineers could have built it, for it is a masterpiece of the handyman and are not sailors the handymen of the world? Some day Heath Robinson will portray that Portsmouth roller and at once he will be accused of going beyond all reasonable bounds in humorous ingenuity. Yet the 'heavy roller' is in use, and it is to me, a delight of a most delightful city.

PRIESTLEY CUP DAY

AUGUST Bank Holiday is the high noon of the cricketing season. In first-class matches old rivals meet again on fields alive with enduring memories of battles lost and won, and there is scarcely a club in the country without its annual fixture as one of the high-lights of the year.

For Bradford people Bank Holiday Monday is Priestley Cup Final Day, and nowhere in the country is greater cricket enthusiasm displayed than at Park Avenue on this occasion. The crowd falls nothing short of that for a county match, and the play itself is invariably worthy of the festival. Great names have been included in these finals, and a Priestley Cup medal is a cherished possession of some cricketers who have written their names on the cricket scrolls of both sides of the world.

It was at Park Avenue in one of these finals that I was first enraptured by C. B. Llewellyn, of South Africa and Hampshire. I suppose that in those days a South African to me was a strange, mystical being from entirely another world, and something in Llewellyn's swarthy countenance captured and held my imagination. I know that for years afterwards I made each Saturday a long and perilous journey

to the Undercliffe cricket ground, and that when
Llewellyn was not in action my interest in the game
underwent a temporary evaporation.

I recall quite clearly that Llewellyn was always
regarded as the 'danger man' by his team's
opponents, and though I cannot remember whether
or not he brought his side to victory—

" When this new planet first swam within my ken,"

I do recollect considerable success attending his
sturdy left-hand batting.

There were great names in the Bradford League
in those days, and almost every team boasted a man
who played a part in first-class cricket during happier
years. Sydney Barnes, I know, was wreaking havoc
for Saltaire, and he, too, figures in a cup-tie memory
of mine. His side was suffering a steady, sure defeat,
and Barnes, for once, was impotent.

On the pavilion balcony one whose celebrations
had been a little premature held forth in highest
glee at Barnes' discomfiture. 'Hundred wickets,
has he? Huh, he can't bowl our lads out. I tell you,
he's beat—he don't know where to drop the next,'
and I rather fancy he leaned over the rails and
strongly advised Barnes to put his sweater on,
'Because you'll never get 'em out.'

It must have been in 1919 that Undercliffe were
victors in another memorable match. I feel sure that
county cricket had been resumed, because George
Gunn was released to play in this final, and the buzz

of expectancy as he came beneath the sunshine to the middle rings in my ears as I write.

And in the very first over, I am almost certain, Gunn was out, caught at short-leg in protecting his face from a high-kicking ball. Oh, the shock, the thrill, the fascination of that moment. But Llewellyn must have come to the rescue again, for I am nearly sure that Undercliffe filed past for their medals at the end of the day.

Everybody who was anybody in Bradford cricket was present at Park Avenue for the Priestley Cup Final. It was a partisan crowd, sharply divided into two camps, but a friendly, jolly crowd for all that. Two rows in front of me a man was having difficulty with a bottle of lemonade—you remember those stupid bottles with a glass marble as a stopper—and he seemed fated to go thirsty for lack of strength or ingenuity. But the cricket did not demand our attention for every instant, and there was soon an offer from immediately behind, 'Here, let me have it; I can open those for you.'

The bottle was gratefully passed over, but proved a tougher proposition than expected. However, dogged and a Sandow thumb did the trick, and 'Swish'—out the foaming liquid shot, most of it upon the man in front.

'I'm awfully sorry, old man; no idea it would come out like that.'

'That's all right, but this is a new suit.'

Greatly daring, the expert essayed to open another bottle and a great roar of laughter announced a similar result. This was, naturally, rather too much for the new-suited gentleman, and he expressed himself forcibly on the subject of 'babies who must have ginger-pop', but the feelings of the crowd were against him and he turned to concentrate once more upon the cricket just in time to receive the full benefit of the third bottle. Memory fails me here. Doubtless I was led away lest my young ears be sullied with what was not for me to know.

There was no going home before the end of these matches. When the last wicket fell, we surged upon the ground and clustered as near the pavilion wall as we could get to see the cup presented and watch each hero take his medal. They were all heroes then, and there was no greater ambition among us boys than one day to step up for a Priestley Cup medal of our own. Well, some of them, no doubt, attained their heart's desire, but most of us must envy always and listen to the stories told of how the match was lost and won.

I know one cricketer whose Priestley Cup medal lies buried somewhere on the Blackpool sands, lost by its winner in trying vainly to teach an unworthy son something of the magic in the father. The memento is no more, but the story never palls with telling, and August Bank Holiday to me is always Priestley Cup Day.

THE BEST OF IT

A GREAT innings or a fine piece of bowling is something more than an athletic event, both to the cricketer concerned and to those whose privilege it is to see. Such feat is a spiritual experience which lingers long after stumps have been drawn for the day, long after the last sun has faded from the summer sky, long after youth has gone and only dreams remain to stir the blood of waning years.

When a great batsman achieves his destiny he does something more than make runs in a particularly attractive or praiseworthy manner; he brings into the world something that was not there before and, moreover, something that cannot pass away any more than it can be repeated. He is no less a creative artist than is a musician who, though he plays familiar chords upon a familiar instrument, yet brings originality to his work because of his own personality.

The infallible test of greatness is the universality of its appeal. True greatness transcends all ulterior considerations and lives because of the shining life within it. A country at war with Italy does not deny the genius of 'The Last Supper'. So a great innings or a great piece of bowling carries men above local patriotism and brings them to praise and wonder because they cannot help themselves.

Not a man on the Melbourne ground but grew above himself in undiluted admiration when Sydney Barnes took five Australian wickets for 6 runs at the beginning of a Test match.   Though Australia were going to destruction almost over by over, yet there was nothing but delight in the heart of every watcher at the sight of perhaps the greatest bowling performance of all time.   The genius of Barnes carried people above minor loyalties and brought them to kinship in their appreciation of an everlasting experience.

When Hammond made his 100 against All-India, he, too, took us away from an encounter between England and the Indians, carried us beyond considerations of this result and that effect to realms we know but rarely yet can always understand.   The Indians themselves, the very bowlers and fieldsmen who strove earnestly and well to bring about his downfall, were first to pay tribute to Hammond.   His batsmanship melted all envy, transcended all wondering, and brought beauty and satisfaction everywhere.

I warrant that never did the Indians feel despair or distress steal upon them while Hammond passed along his noble way; being cricketers, they must have rejoiced in what Hammond gave to them, for they could share the raptures, even as we who watched could share.

Scoreboard details, the ticking of the clock, the

meaning of it all were beyond consideration. We lived in a world of cricket without it formalities as an artist sometimes lives in a world of light beyond mere colour and design.

I suppose that most of us have had the boyhood fancies that took us home, after seeing our heroes, in a mood of determining emulation. We always feel more capable of getting runs or taking wickets when we have recently seen the feats accomplished to our satisfaction. Yet I doubt if we ever fancy ourselves in imitation of the truly great performances; then we do not need to picture ourselves in the position of our heroes, for the desire to equal is primarily the desire to know the feeling of success; then we have shared in the feat itself, then we have known the spiritual excitement of amazing achievement.

Does the musician in movements of rhapsody know greater stimulation than the listener perfectly attuned to his mood? Is the act of performance of any consideration compared with the emanating spiritual aura? Afterwards, I daresay, reflection brings greater joy to the performer than the watcher could ever know, but in the actual hour the greatness is everywhere to be equally shared by all.

That is why cricket is so dear, so precious a game, to us, for it can give its greatest moments to each one of us who loves it. We do not have to count the figures or mark the occasion of the truly great performance. We know it to be perfection because we can feel it within our bones, because we can share it and treasure it to the end of our time. That is why we cannot afford to smile in patient scepticism at those who tell of the glories of yesterday. We must remember that what they have seen they have shared, and that unless we, too, have known something of their feelings from our own experiences we cannot hope to understand their enthusiasms.

If we watch cricket for long enough, watch it closely enough, we shall know its greatest gifts, though awkwardness be our own bowling companion and stupidity our partner at the crease. Such batting as Hammond gave us on a July day makes cricketers of us all; it needs no criticism, requires no words of praise. It is, and that is sufficient; if we can appreciate its appeal we are true cricketers all.

A DAY AND A HALF

WEDNESDAY, 1ST AUGUST, 1935

MORNINGS will come and mornings will go, but it will surely be a long, long time before Huddersfield sees such another morning as this one. Between 11.30 and lunch time, beneath a fair sky, with the sun reflecting from a polished wicket, thirteen players completed their innings and collected 70 runs between them. Less than twenty-four hours ago some of us sat at Old Trafford and thought bowlers never likely to take another wicket.

Read and Nichols were magnificent this morning, and Lancashire would be prepared to pay half the season's profits for the loan of them over the week-end. Nichols galloped down hill, all elbows and feet, his hair gleaming as brightly as the pitch, and Read, even more angular in action, ran and bowled still faster from the other end. Yorkshire's batsmen were routed, scattered, nonplussed, and shockingly dismissed; only Wood made double figures, and he might well have been out first ball. The spectators passed through the stages of wild alarm, distressed seriousness, and bitter mirth. Purchasers of lunch editions in Leeds, Bradford, and Sheffield hurried off to consult oculists, or write to editors concerning the unreliability of stop-press news.

In short, the incredible happened, and Yorkshire were put out in an hour's play for 31 runs. All through the luncheon interval telephone bells were ringing for confirmation of the miraculous, and explanation of the catastrophe. Confirmation was easy, and the explanation not too difficult, for the plain truth is that good fast bowling on a fast bowler's wicket where the ball bounced high instead of drifting sullenly was far too much for batsmen quite unused to such happenings.

The drama began in Read's first over, when a good length ball rose quickly and went from Barber's glove to the gully, and continued almost without cessation until Bowes hit Nichols gently to Rist at cover-point.

In Read's second over, Sellers tried to turn a straight ball to leg, edged it towards point, Wilcox made a good catch, and Yorkshire were 6 for two. One ball later they were 6 for three, for Leyland had just time to touch the ball before it removed his leg stump, and the only addition to the score was a no-ball when Gibb was caught low down at short fine leg.

Nichols was bowling far too well to miss reward altogether, and at 9 he had the fifth and sixth wickets with successive balls, Sutcliffe being caught at the wicket and Hutton clean bowled. Wood failed to give him the hat-trick, despite a desperate effort to 'get a touch', and a moment later he became one of the principal run-getters with a two past mid-off.

The seventh wicket actually multiplied the total by three, for Wood had a boundary from each bowler, but even so, the board showed 27 for seven when Turner was caught by Sheffield wide on the off side.

Fisher missed one ball and was bowled by the second, and, still at 27, Wood played forward for the ball to fly from the inside edge to provide another good catch at square-leg. Bowes put his left foot towards mid-on and hit a boundary past mid-off from his first ball, and the innings was over at half-past twelve. The bowling figures must, of course, be given in full, for they are worthy of attention, but they cannot do full justice to the life and fire of the attack, and they do not show the excellence of the Essex fielding.

	o.	m.	r.	w.
Nichols .	6·4	2	17	4
Read . .	6	1	11	6

The Yorkshire attack was as the mild lapping of a Mediterranean tide to a North Atlantic tempest compared with the Essex bowling. If this was a fast bowler's wicket, Yorkshire had no fast bowler and the best they could do was a little make-believe when Wood stood five yards back to take Verity.

At five minutes past one, when Essex were 24, Verity bowled Sheffield, and before the Yorkshire total had been passed Wilcox, cutting at a wide ball from Turner, was caught at the wicket. To complete a riotous morning, Cutmore was caught by Wood off the last ball before lunch, and the players hurried away to discuss matters out of the sun.

In the afternoon Fisher completed his over by bowling O'Connor, much to that batsman's surprise, but thereafter Yorkshire bade a fond farewell to success, and toiled and moiled with ever-growing hopelessness and distress.

Rist, it is true, got himself out at 65 by an over-indulgence in an admirable hook, but by that time he alone had made more than all the Yorkshiremen put together, and when Nichols and Belle came into partnership fieldsmen and bowlers experienced all the miseries of frustrated ambition for hour upon hour. Belle started badly, and might have been out half a dozen times in his first ten minutes, but he was not, and such introductions usually mean long acquaintanceships.

Nichols had already been in close contact with the wicket and found it suitable for bowling, but he had his pads on now and was prepared to point out its suitability for batting—Essex batting.

Slowly at first, and then more easily, Nichols and Belle overcame such merits as existed in the Yorkshire attack, and by 3.15 the 100 was up. Having tasted the delights of a six with a leg hit off Turner, Nichols found the entertainment to his liking and hit Verity out of sight beyond long-on, coming to his 50 at four o'clock with another boundary from Leyland.

In one hour and thirty-five minutes—agonizing minutes not eased for Yorkshire by the fact that Sellers at square leg dropped a hard catch from Belle—the partnership became worth 100 and at tea-time Essex were 179, Nichols 75 and Belle 36.

Belle was in no hurry for his 50, and Nichols left him so far behind that there was but twenty-five minutes between Belle's 50 and Nichols' century, and long before the realization of either accomplishment Yorkshire had become a disorganized rabble with stumping chances missed, catches dropped, and misfielding so common as to draw forth no comment.

To them the day's disaster must have seemed limitless, and when three hours and ten minutes after his arrival Belle pulled Leyland to Verity at mid-wicket to end a stand of 174, it was only to admit Eastman to the wicket, and Eastman promptly proceeded to make 23 runs in ten minutes, two of his hits being tremendous straight sixes.

Almost from the beginning Nichols was contemptuously triumphant; he knew inwardly that the day was to be his, and neither escapes nor unpleasant possibilities caused him the least concern. His strokes were his own, made in his own time and at his own discretion, and in no way depending upon the dictation of the bowlers. When he wanted to pull, he pulled, and when his spirit so urged him, he drove; some shots counted four, sometimes fieldsmen were in the way. Nichols was indifferent.

Not until long after six o'clock did Bowes, on a fast bowler's day, take a wicket, and then Eastman, mishitting a drive, was caught at deep mid-off, and 15 runs later Smith (P.) was bowled, playing lazily back. Nichols went on to the last five minutes, with two 6's and fifteen 4's to his credit, when an intended drive found a home in third man's hands.

Yorkshire may derive what consolation they can from the fact that they will not have to field tomorrow, and by the going down of the sun they were utterly weary; time is a great healer, and some time perhaps this nightmare will fade.

YORKSHIRE
First Innings

Sutcliffe, c Sheffield, b Nicholls	4
Barber, c Wilcox, b Read	1
A. B. Sellers, c Wilcox, b Read	2
Leyland, b Read	0
P. A. Gibb, c Rist, b Read	0
Turner, c Sheffield, b Read	4
Hutton, b Nichols	0
Wood, c Read, b Nichols	13
Fisher, b Read	0
Verity, not out	0
Bowes, c Rist, b Nichols	4
B. 1, l.b. 1, n.b. 1	3
Total	31

ESSEX
First Innings

Sheffield, b Verity	5
Rist, c Gibb, b Verity . . .	35
Wilcox, c Wood, b Turner . . .	2
Cutmore, c Wood, b Fisher . . .	2
O'Connor, b Fisher	0
Nichols, c Hutton, b Bowes . .	146
B. H. Belle, c Verity, b Leyland ' . .	63
Eastman, c Gibb, b Bowes . .	23
Smith (P.), b Bowes	5
Smith (R.), not out	16
H. D. Read, st Wood, b Verity . .	0
B. 24, l.b. 13	37
Total	334

BOWLING ANALYSIS
YORKSHIRE
First Innings

	o.	m.	r.	w.		o.	m.	r.	w.
Nichols	6·4	2	17	4	Read	6	1	11	6

Read bowled one no-ball.

ESSEX
First Innings

	o.	m.	r.	w.		o.	m.	r.	w.
Bowes .	37	8	77	3	Fisher .	25	5	62	2
Turner .	16	2	41	1	Leyland .	5	1	38	1
Verity .	24·2	4	79	3					

THURSDAY

By an innings and 204 runs Essex deprived Yorkshire of an unbeaten championship record and were free to leave Huddersfield before lunch on this, the second day of the match.

The victory was utterly complete, for in batting, bowling, fielding, and even wicket-keeping, Yorkshire were tremendously outplayed. To Nichols the game must be ever memorable, for rarely, indeed, does a cricketer take eleven wickets and score 146

in a day and a half. He and Read were not, perhaps,
so devastatingly unkind this morning as they were
yesterday, but the bowling figures are not altogether
reliable, for many runs came from that part of the
bat not designed for regular use, and any shot
missing a fieldsman counted four.

To lose, even so monstrously as this, is not perhaps
a vital matter to Yorkshire, but far more disturbing
is the sorry show put up by the batsmen against
bowling that was always fast enough to earn full
reward from a fast bowler's wicket, and the complete inability of the Yorkshire bowlers to find virtue
in the same piece of turf.

Had Yorkshire recovered manfully to-day, we
might have believed that the wicket was only lively
at the game's beginning, and that the mediocrity of
the Yorkshire attack was not all inherent, but Nichols
and Read proved again that pace and life could have
brought adequate reward at any time, and, clearly,
the fault in no way lay in the stars but in ourselves.

Essex showed us great cricket in this match, and
we account them our masters, passing on in the determination that this game of ours has infinite variety
and that her charms whilst honest men change into
flannels will be abiding always. We came to Fartown
this morning not knowing what to expect but feeling
in the bottom of our hearts that Essex held all the
cards and that the day's interest would lie in the
playing of them.

The methods were direct and to the point, for in Nichol's first over, with a single score by each batsman, Sutcliffe pushed forward at an outswinger and edged a low catch to first slip. There is a legend of a gentleman going to see Beckett fight Carpentier, leaning down to put his hat beneath the seat and rising to find the fight all over. It is highly probable that many people on the ground had not thoroughly settled themselves before Yorkshire's first wicket went down to-day.

With that warning given, concentration became acute, and the game progressed in that breathless silence which means constant expectancy and not a little desperation.

Barber did well within the range of Yorkshire batsmen thus far, for he had 14 runs in one over from Read, a 2 past mid-off, two boundaries from good shots in front of and behind point, and a third 4 which passed through the hands of the wicket-keeper on its electric way.

At 21, with half an hour gone, he was bowled with some reason to be sorry for himself; Nichols dropped one well short of a length and Barber prepared to hook, but the ball kept deceitfully low and the stumps were gigantically shattered. Barber was perhaps unwise to consider a hook shot in the circumstances, but he was in no way to blame for the ball failing to rise to expectations.

Sellers was always in trouble; several times Nichols threw up his arms in anticipation of the ball finding the edge of the bat, but Sellers did not die that way, and Nichols had to bowl at the stumps to get him leg-before at 22.

Leyland broke a bat so thoroughly that it was taken from the field in two pieces, but the new one brought him no success at all, for at 24 he was clean bowled and 'Ichabod' was written large all over Yorkshire.

Gibb and Turner, by fair means and fortunate, added 19 runs to the microscopic total, and actually persuaded Essex to a bowling change, Eastman going on for Read at 30—(a Yorkshire voice suggested that Nichols, too, might well be rested) but good fours to fine leg by both batsmen were no more than scratches upon the diamond-hard surface of the Essex victory, and, after a skied shot that fell clear of everyone, Turner's leg-stump went mournfully down.

Gibb's final boundary was off the edge from Eastman, and at 48 Nichols had him lbw. Hutton stayed until 12.30, but he could not score, and achieved a distinction gained by more famous men than he when Nichols took his sixth wicket of the morning.

By this time Read had come back into the attack, and Wood, if not exactly welcoming him, had two uppish boundaries past point to make the total very nearly the equal of the minutes gone by. By the time he had reached 19, Wood was acknowledged the chief scorer of each Yorkshire innings, but with one or two more cheerful hits we bade him farewell, not without affection, as Nichols spread his stumps fanwise with a ball of lovely length.

Fisher got off the mark, and then turned Read into Rist's hands at square-leg, and when Bowes had hit four 4's, two above the slips, and one that nearly brought untimely demise to the bowler, a slip catch finished the match at five minutes to one with Yorkshire again out for less than 100.

YORKSHIRE

First Innings			Second Innings	
Sutcliffe, c Sheffield, b Nichols		4	c Eastman, b Nichols	1
Barber, c Wilcox, b Read	.	1	b Nichols . .	18
A. B. Sellers, c Wilcox, b Read .		2	lbw, b Nichols	2
Leyland, b Read . .	.	0	b Read . .	2
P. A. Gibb, c Rist, b Read	.	0	lbw (n), b Nichols .	11
Turner, c Sheffield, b Read	.	4	b Nichols . .	13
Hutton, b Nichols . .	.	0	lbw, b Nichols .	0
Wood, c Read, b Nichols .	.	13	b Nichols . .	24
Fisher, b Read . .	.	0	c Rist, b Read .	2
Verity, not out . .	.	0	c Smith (P), b Read	6
Bowes, c Rist, b Nichols .	.	4	not out . .	19
B. 1, l.b. 1, n.b. 1 .	.	3	L.b. . .	1
Total . . .	.	31	Total . .	99

ESSEX
First Innings

Sheffield, b Verity .	.	.	.	.	5
Rist, c Gibb, b Verity .	.	.	.	35
Wilcox, c Wood, b Turner .	.	.	.	2
Cutmore, c Wood, b Fisher .	.	.	.	2
O'Connor, b Fisher .	.	.	.	0
Nichols, c Hutton, b Bowes .	.	.		146
B. H. Belle, c Verity, b Leyland .	.	.		63
Eastman, c Gibb, b Bowes .	.	.		23
Smith (P.), b Bowes .	.	.	.	5
Smith (R.), not out .	.	.	.	16
H. D. Read, st Wood, b Verity .	.	.		0
B. 24, l.b. 13 .	.	.	.	37
Total . .	.	.		334

BOWLING ANALYSIS
YORKSHIRE
First Innings

	o.	m.	r.	w.		o.	m.	r.	w.
Nichols	6·4	2	17	4	Read	6	1	11	6

Read bowled one no-ball.

Second Innings

	o.	m.	r.	w.		o.	m.	r.	w.
Nichols	15	3	37	7	Eastman	3	0	10	0
Read	11·4	2	51	3					

ESSEX
First Innings

	o.	m.	r.	w.		o.	m.	r.	w.
Bowes	37	8	77	3	Fisher	25	5	62	2
Turner	16	2	41	1	Leyland	5	1	38	1
Verity	24·2	4	79	3					

Umpires : Chester and Walden.

AN AUGUST DAY

CRICKET's leaves are falling fast, for the autumn of the season is upon us and the fresh green of timid springtime strokes against the turning ball has changed to the bold bright colours of the confidence that has infinite faith in the wicket and knows the burnt turf as a broad polished highway to the boundaries.

In these days a batsman paints his innings in vivid browns and reds and golds and has a final riotous fling before the cold winds sweep him away for the winter and leave his fields chill and desolate, whilst the guardian groundsman repairs the ravages of summer in the brief hours of daylight at his disposal.

Cricket in late August and early September is in tomboyish mood, for the sobering influence of farewell is not yet at hand and every day brings hot sunshine and holiday mood.

Now is the batsman in his element, the major problems of the campaign settled, worries and responsibilities behind him, and new records close at hand. There is leisure here to look and love. The beauty of the game is brightly shining, and its lovely spell is woven tightly round us.

Precious game that brings us each morning, as the sun rides high and gathers strength for a blazing breathless afternoon, to the familiar gates and cheerful 'Good-day to you, Sir', greeting; that bids us pause to gaze upon the players drifting from the cool pavilion shadows, and marvel at the freshness and the sameness of it all; that holds us all day long in watching wonder and unspoken sympathy as brave dreams become realities before our eyes.

Cricket was born in England and is England's own whomsoever may sail the seas to take Ashes and Rubber away from us; cricket is of us, as the very breath in our lungs, makes poets of the incoherent and artists of the artisans.

Not one of us that takes a bat or bowls a ball or watches a game but gives and receives a precious heritage. Cricket takes us from ourselves because we give ourselves to it, and its appeal is permanent and infinite because it is a part of all of us. Its pictures are unending because each one is seen with a different eye and in a different mood.

Cricket's chief attraction is its universality, for poor indeed and unhappy is he who has not at some time in some small way known its joys. Every boy who has defended a lamp-post wicket is in blood brotherhood with Bradman, and knows Hobbs or Sutcliffe as himself raised to and beyond the power of n; every man who has by reflex action or conscious effort flicked a boundary past point knows a thrill of intense physical delight when he sees Woolley bat.

Our sweetest cricketers, whom day by day we applaud and admire, have the happy qualities of human idols, for we, too, have tasted of their wine and shared of their moments, yet never dare aspire to their station.

The cricket of Canterbury or Old Trafford or Lord's is but the cricket of the railway goods yard differently circumstanced and accoutred with more care. A low, swooping slip catch is as beautiful in Brixton as in Bournemouth, just as a swallow makes curving delights of flight round dust-bins and rhododendron bushes alike. Beauty we see in cricket because cricket is beauty, and no alteration of environment can remove an inborn quality.

We praise great cricketers because somewhere within us we can feel their ambitions, understand their ideals, and picture their desires. We know through our own experiences the difficulties, the trials and troubles that beset them, and we can sympathize in failure and share in joyful success.

There is the warmth of comradeship in every ball bowled or every stroke played in cricket. That is why thousands upon thousands will sit patiently beneath the scorching sun until the cool shades of evening and find in each hour something to remember.

It is worse than idle to complain of the ignorance of a cricket crowd; ignorance of detail there may be because of the distance of the prospect, but there is never ignorance of the purpose of the game which is, first and last, the creation of living beauty in a particular medium.

Cricket is ethically independent of the score board, and I have known a crowd enthralled where no scoreboard existed, and had it been present would have told a dull tale. When we read that Hammond has made 170 in an innings of two hours' duration we do not picture it in figures, but in sweeping curves of flannels, brown arms and white bat and the ball making swift patterns across the grass.

When we are told that Larwood has bowled down seven wickets we do not think of flying stumps so much as of pounding feet and a whirling arm circling and circling in magical curve. As cricketers we are all artists, and as artists we are more nearly god-like in our mortality. All this is done for us by a game, a dear, lovely game that will be ours until green fields and sweet sunshine have passed from the earth.

SCARBOROUGH

WHEREVER a pilgrimage through the cricketer's England may begin it must surely end, if the traveller have any sense of the appropriate, at Scarborough in Festival time. There are gathered together for ten days in September all who matter in the cricketing world. To-day's players come for one last battle together before bats and pads are packed mournfully away for the winter; yesterday's players come to sit in the summer's last sunshine and talk over achievements long since written in history: to-morrow's players come to feed the flame of hero-worship and to cajole inspiration and autographs in the most cheerful cricketing feast of the year.

During the Festival Scarborough gives itself over completely to cricket and cricketers. Not to be concerned with cricket in the first days of September is to be an outcast in Scarborough, a stranger in a strange land without reason or justification for existence. There are cricket dances, cricket banquets, cricket celebrations of every possible kind, cricket is first and last in the mind of every public entertainer.

Scarborough Cricket Festival has tradition behind it and would persist now from its own momentum; its patrons are its chief advertisement, for they come year after year to meet each other and to tell the same stories. Yet Scarborough made the Cricket Festival, not the Cricket Festival Scarborough, for the town has attractions outside cricket and unconnected with it. It is no upstart of public fancy, no tinsel town of purely summer satisfaction. Scarborough has life of its own and has had from the days when Norman William came so devastatingly into the North Country.

High upon the cliff that separates the bays stands Scarborough's castle, built in Norman times upon the site of an earlier fortification. To-day those who climb the steep pathway can find little more than a ruined keep, torn and desolate through long disuse and the ravages of a thousand storms. Within the remnants of the great fireplace birds find sanctuary, and only the narrow windows and walls of enormous thickness tell the tale of the strength and dignity of what was once an important military house. There are many medieval castles in a better state of preservation than that at Scarborough, but few can have more striking setting or be regarded with such affection by those who look upon the sight of it as a sign of a pleasure consummated.

From the castle hill you look north and south to the two lovely bays that make up the town. North, the foreground gives you hotels and boarding houses with the cliff falling swiftly to a crowded bathing beach backed by Peasholm Park and a notable

open-air theatre, with the coastline beyond running
a scarred way to Scalby and Whitby. South, the
bay is wider and smooth, and nestling beneath the
protective castle hill is the busy harbour whence
come and go the trawlers that seek a dangerous
living in a sea of notoriously uncertain temper.

Beyond the harbour and the foreshore lies the
resort of fashion, the playground of the idle. The
Spa has genuine curative waters and to them owes its
origin, but the Spa is now the centre of Scarborough's
holiday life and the waters are no more than a
curiosity. On the Spa there is good music and dance
music (these in enumeration rather than in any
spirit of comparison) throughout the day; it has
pleasant walks upon the cliff-side, a concert hall and
theatre, is in fact, a little world of its own. In the
morning it is favoured, in the afternoon it is busy,
in the evening it has no rival.

Above the Spa, beyond the hotels that look across
the sea from South Cliff top, you come to Oliver's
Mount, whence, so legend would have us believe,
Cromwell once made assault upon the castle. To
climb Oliver's Mount on foot is half a day's journey,
for the path is winding and steep, but even that toil
is amply repaid in the end, for from where Scarborough has built memorial to her fallen you may
find as exquisite a view as imagination can conjure.
The War Memorial has become a landmark to the
traveller; from the inland road long before the smell

of the sea has reached you the memorial comes into view, and instinctively your pace increases with journey's end at hand. The first glimpse of Oliver's Mount is both a spur and a sedative, for Scarborough calls urgently and at the same time announces welcome proximity.

Once visited, Scarborough takes hold of you inexorably; one visit leads to another, until the succession has turned to ritual and the spell is laid never to be broken. Always you leave Scarborough with something still to be seen or done; always you return to rejoice in familiar sights and repeat fond achievements. Scarborough is always new yet never changes. The daily business insists upon constant variety, yet the years have brought a stable mellowness. You see the trawlers unload as you have seen them unload hundreds of times before, yet there is novelty in this particular catch; you go to see (and hear) the Scottish herring girls in their annual visit, and note what you missed before. As evening comes you stroll towards the Spa and find the familiar outlines of the castle tinged with new light, clothed in yet another atmosphere. Scarborough, as much as any town in the world, has personality, and it is that personality which brings you again and again to her lovely and precious scenes.

THE PAVILION LIBRARY